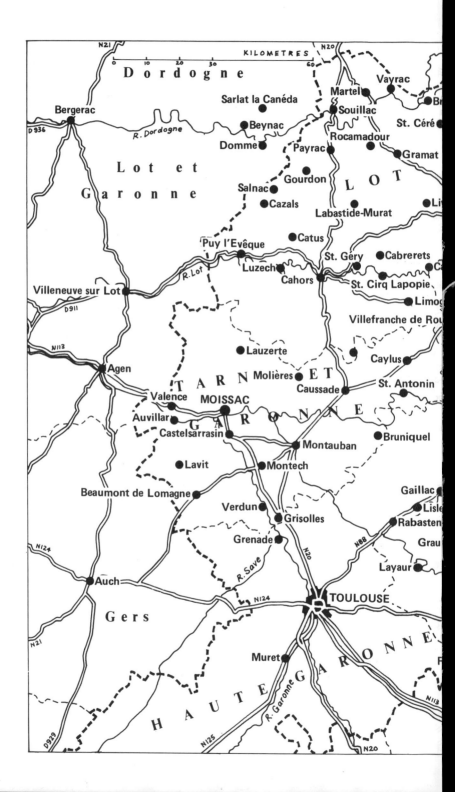

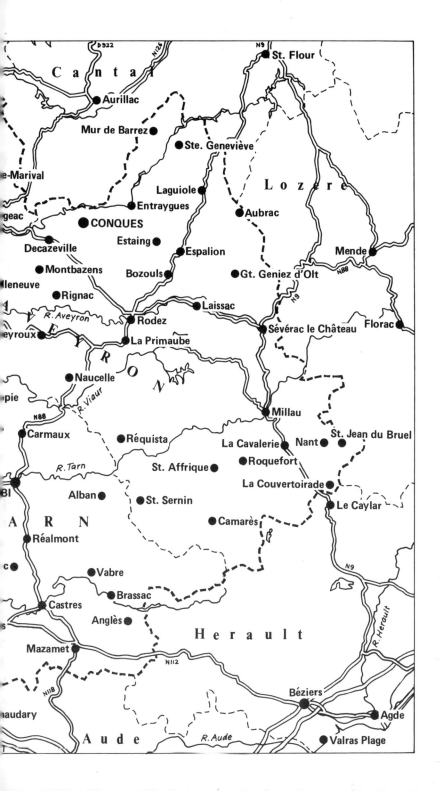

History, People and Places
Beyond the Dordogne

Pont Valentré at Cahors

HISTORY, PEOPLE AND PLACES

BEYOND THE DORDOGNE

Neil Lands

SPURBOOKS LIMITED

Published by Spurbooks Limited
6 Parade Court, Bourne End, Buckinghamshire

ISBN 0 904978 88 5

Designed and produced by
Mechanick Exercises, London

Typesetting by Inforum, Portsmouth

Printed in Great Britain by
Tonbridge Printers Limited
Peach Hall Works, Tonbridge, Kent

Contents

Illustrations

Acknowledgements

The author and publishers would like to acknowledge the assistance of the following people in the preparation of this book: Pauline Hallam of the French Government Tourist Office, London; Patrick Goyet and Elfie Tran in Toulouse; Bernard Lucas in Montauban; Monique Labonnete of the Association des Gîtes du Quercy, Cahors; The Syndicates of Rodez, Moissac and Montauban; L'Hotel Chapon Fin, Moissac; The London Library.

1

Beyond the Dordogne

Every intelligent man has two countries; his own and France. Or so they say. Over the centuries, people have had a lot to say about France and it seems only reasonable to ask why, in a wide and diverse continent, so much love and attention should fall on one particular country.

When Strabo, the Greek geographer, was surveying the Roman Empire in the time of Augustus, he wrote that Gaul was a land *"designed by nature to meet the needs and wants of man."*

Much later, in the 18th century, Talleyrand wrote that the French, the fortunate inhabitants of this happy land, seemed more than most to value the *douceur de vivre*, the sweetness of life.

Well, things have changed a lot in the last two hundred years, and while in material things the lot of many people has undoubtedly improved, few would deny that the *douceur de vivre* has turned a little sour.

Yet, that said, France has something, and the object of this book is to try and find it.

We will not, I believe, find a pleasing style of life in the big cities. If it still exists at all it will be in the country, away from the bustle and the noise, and here, ever fortunate, France is well equipped, for it is a large country, infinitely varied, beautiful, and historically appealing.

The grass is not greener on the other side of the Channel and yet, ... and yet .... Well, we shall see.

* * * *

I have always wanted to travel on a map that had "*Here be Dragons*" written on it, or at any rate, in places as unfrequented as possible by my fellow countrymen. There are, as far as I know, no dragons in the regions beyond the Dordogne, but there is practically everything else.

I crossed the Dordogne at Argentat. The river here, in late May, was wide, swollen with the late spring rains, deep chocolate-brown in colour, heavy with sediment and not a pretty sight at all. Dr. Johnson once remarked that France was worse than Scotland in everything except climate, and everyone knows what the Doctor thought of Scotland, but France, even in the rain, is not without compensations. I parked the car on the far side of the bridge and walked back, hunched up against the rain, to have a coffee in the warm little restaurant on the quay. Once inside, and steaming gently, I got out my map and studied it.

If you do likewise, you will see to the west of Bordeaux, the course of a mighty river. It rises in the Auvergne and flows south and west for three hundred miles until it flows into the Garonne, and thus into the Atlantic. This river, the Dordogne, is the northern boundary of this book.

The English, as all the world must know, love the Dordogne, both the river itself, and the *département* to which it gives a name, and they flock there in increasing numbers. It may be the climate, which is agreeable, it may be the food of Périgord, which is delicious, it may even be the fact that it marks the most southern point at which you can still easily receive the B.B.C., but whatever the reason, the Dordogne is a mecca for *les Anglais*.

Beyond the Dordogne, on the other hand, the English are comparatively rare, or perhaps just less visible, but it is not a desire to avoid the company of my countrymen that sends me to the land beyond the river.

"England! With all thy faults I love thee still!
I said at Calais and have not forgot it;"

The basic reason for the trip was to take a break between writing about Burgundy and Ile de France, and enjoy some splendid scenery.

Different people, mercifully, like different things. "It would be a poor place if we were all alike" as my old Scots granny used to say. The country south of the Dordogne has little or no unity, historic, political or geographic, but you can get there easily. It is very beautiful and there are no crowds. I work in the City and get tired of crowds, and besides, it is not really as disparate as all that.

Patrick Goyet, a friend in Toulouse, looked very doubtful when I told him of my project. As he pointed out, it covers two areas, firstly the *'Pays Cathar'*, the country of the Albigensians around Toulouse and Albi, and secondly, what is really a frontier area, the old war-zone between the Auvergne and the territory of the Counts of Toulouse, a fragmented area, composed of parts of Quercy, most of the Rouergue, and the southern Cantal. The countryside everywhere is delightful and there are no present frontiers and few barriers to travel beyond the occasional flooded road or rockfall.

This book is, I hope, a lighthearted account of a tour through provincial France. In other books, I have stayed within the boundaries of some specific region, such as Burgundy, the Dordogne, or Languedoc-Roussillon. In this one, although much of it lies in the modern region of Midi-Pyrenees, I shall have to skate about a bit. Well, so be it!

"Tell me a story
That nobody knows,
And show me a Country,
Where nobody goes . . ."

That scrap of verse gives the objects of this book, and within reason, we will maintain them. However, the area is not completely unknown and is full of interest.

Toulouse, the largest town, is the fourth city of France, with a long and eventful history, while Agen, Cahors and Rodez are hardly insignificant provincial capitals. For the people to throng our stage we have a host of characters, political and artistic, ranging from Gambetta and Jean Juarés to Ingres and Lautrec, who,

17

while not unknown are still perhaps less familiar to the foreigner than they should be.

If you will now take a little time to study the endpaper map, you will see that the area of our journey is bordered to the north by the Dordogne, and has another river, the Garonne, marking the boundary to the west on a line between Toulouse and Agen. In the south, the area stops in the Espinouse, and a little further west at the heights of the Montagne Noir. At their furthest point, we head north, skirting Lozére, across the *causses*, to the Rouergue, the remote Aubrac, and Cantal, and we finally leave the area by crossing the Truyére, the historic boundary in the North between Auvergne and Rouergue.

This is a large area, some thousands of square miles, and very varied, but there are two linking features which will appear continually in this book. The first is the River Aveyron, which rises near Sévérac in the east and flows west towards Moissac. The second is the great medieval pilgrim route from Le Puy to Santiago de Compostella in Spain, which enters our region near Conques, and runs south across the country towards Toulouse. For great natural beauty, and considerable variety, the area covered by this book is unmatched, and one way to see it is to follow the pilgrim road.

For the rest, we can let cohesion go hang, and wander about

Road to Compostella

through these beautiful old provinces of Quercy and Rouergue, along the river valleys of the Lot and the Tarn, and a score of lesser rivers to see what there is to see, beyond the Dordogne.

* * * *

"Good beginnings make good endings" as my old Scots granny, making her farewell appearance in this book, used to say. Careful preparation for a journey is not only advisable, but enjoyable, extending a summer journey back into the winter. The first requirement is good maps. I rely firstly, for getting there, on the Michelin Red 'Grandes Routes', scale 1 cm : 10 km. Once in the area, I recommend the Institut Geographique National Carte Touristique, scale 1 cm : 2.5 km. and for this book you will need four: No. 11 (Auvergne), No. 10 (Bordelais), No. 13 (Pyrénées-Occidentale), and No. 14 (Pyrénées-Languedoc). The 'Cartes Touristique' illustrate all the worthwhile historic and scenic attractions in the area, and the scale is large enough to show the smallest routes from one to the other.

No traveller to France should fail to equip himself with two annual publications, the 'red Michelin' and the 'Guide des Logis et Auberges Rurales de France'. This last, which is less well known than it should be, gives information on over three thousand small, family-run hotels, all over France. They are, in general, moderately priced and well run. The 'Guide des Relais Routiers' lists those cafés and restaurants frequented by French lorry drivers, establishments where the food is often good and always plentiful.

This may seem like a considerable outlay on maps and publications, but the saving in hotel and restaurant bills is a worthwhile compensation. If money is no object, and you speak a little French, you might care to add the Gault-Millau gastronomic guide, which lists good hotels and restaurants and, unlike Michelin, also describes their setting, service and ambiance. For the cognoscenti the Gault-Millau is a must.

If you speak no French, then remember that the Briton abroad always has two languages: English, and louder English!

19

The wise traveller in France, wander as he will, usually follows three basic rules; he travels on D-roads, he stays in 'Logis' hotels, and he eats from the Michelin, and if you do the same you won't go far wrong.

Getting beyond the Dordogne is the first task, and since the most northern point lies some four hundred miles from the Channel, it is best to cross at night to Le Havre or Cherbourg, and by arriving at the French port early in the morning, you get most of the trip disposed of in the first day. From the northern ports of Calais or Boulogne, it is perhaps best to pick up the autoroute near Arras for the run south, leaving it to cut off west at Tournus or Mâcon, but you can avoid the autoroute, which is boring and expensive by using the Norman ports, and head south through either Poitiers or Limoges, or along the banks of the Loire, through Nevers and Moulins. Whichever of these three routes you choose, try whenever possible, to get off the main 'N' (National) roads, crowded with other cars and articulated *camions*, and on to any available 'D' 'Departmental' one. These are just as fast, much less crowded, and will often take you through some little-known and very beautiful areas. A good traveller always uses the most minor road available, except perhaps in the mountains.

The next decision is when to go, and if there is a choice, any time in summer other than late July and August is to be preferred. The area has a long summer, from early May through to October, and the spring and autumn are, to my mind, as enjoyable as high summer, when the area is burnt yellow by the blasting sun and a heat-haze obscures those great, vast views which are the real joy of this part of the world.

The area can be visited on foot, for it is great walking country, reached either by train or plane, but in this book I assume a car and a few weeks holiday. You should, however, decide to abandon the car and walk whenever possible, and with this decided, and a little money, it's time to go.

* * * *

Bourgeneuf, on the Creuse, was the first stop, and a town I had long wanted to visit. It belonged, in the early Middle Ages, to the Military Order of the Hospital, and it was a Grand Master of the Order, Pierre d'Aubusson, who fortified the town in the late 15th century to shelter his captive, the Turkish Prince Zizim, or Djem, brother of the Sultan Bajazet II. The Prince had led an unsuccessful coup against his brother, and fled to take shelter with the Order when it failed. Bajazet paid the Knights 40,000 ducats a year to keep him in captivity, and d'Aubusson used part of the money to found the tapestry works at his birthplace, five miles away. The tapestries of Aubusson were, and remain, examples of the finest craftsmanship.

Aubusson is only one of several French towns to give name and birth to a textile. Shakespeare's Hamlet stabbed Polonious behind the products of Arras, while wearing, no doubt, a shirt trimmed with cambric, imported of course from Cambrai, and had his mother, Gertrude, mourned the act she would have concealed the fact behind a veil from the weavers of Tulle.

Apart from memories of Aubusson and Djem, who later suffered the not uncommon fate of being poisoned by the Borgias, Bourgeneuf is a nice town, quite small, with less than four thousand people, and one excellent hotel, '*Le Commerce*', in the centre, ideal for a tour of the town. You can visit the Tour Zizim, where the prince lived in luxurious captivity, and inspect the relics of the Knights in the town museum.

Bourgeneuf lies in the *département* of the Creuse, on the edge of the Limousin, and from there our route lies due south, on D-roads of course, out of the Creuse and into Vienne. This is a good road through beautiful flower-strewn water meadows and across ridges that give fine views over the hills. Peyrat-le-Château, a town that entirely surrounds a small lake, is the touring centre in this part of the world, with lots of hotels and a fine camp-site.

From Peyrat, the road climbs steadily through wooded hills and past many, too many, empty houses, each a silent witness to the massive depopulation which afflicts rural France, and so out of Vienne, into Corréze.

By about 11 o'clock it was time to think about lunch, which in my case usually consists of a picnic with wine, cheese, fruit and bread. The *epicier* at La Celle provided me with three of these and the lady in charge, having no bread, directed me to the bakery. "It's at the back of the wine store" she explained. "The owner is an old bachelor and as you know, they can be a bit funny, but he will sell you some."

The bakery took a lot of finding, and only after climbing over a few crates and hammering on several doors, did I find the right entrance. The crusty old bachelor turned out to be ten years younger than me! "If you are not married by twenty, everyone here thinks you are peculiar" he explained. The bakery was pitch dark, but as my eyes got used to the gloom I saw that it was full of menfolk, muttering darkly about women, and waiting to collect their bread. I'd never been inside a French bakery before and was most intrigued to see how the loaves, of varying lengths and shapes, are actually baked. Clearly normal baking tins are useless for the long thin *baguettes*. The baker spread out a damp sheet of canvas on a large flat tin tray, and then ruffled it up. The dough was then laid out in strips between the folds, and the whole lot slid into the tin.

The waiting period was whiled away with glasses of wine, and we all emerged, blinking like a woodful of owls, each clutching a hot, crisp baguette, and heading hurriedly for lunch.

The road south to Tulle, has several lakes and reservoirs to picnic beside and this avoids stopping in Tulle itself, which is a much modernised town on the banks of the Corréze. If you should decide to stop there, then you can dine well at the '*Toque-Blanche*' or the *Restaurant de la Gare*.

* * * *

Any traveller through Southern France will acquire an acquaintance with the three great wars which ravaged the region. The first was the Albigensian Crusade, which the King of France used as a pretext to destroy the Counts of Toulouse. This lasted from about 1200 to 1250. In the next century came '*the time of the English*', the Hundred Years War, which lasted, with gaps, from 1346 to 1453.

Finally, in the 16th century, came the various Wars of Religion, when the countryside was a battlefield between the forces of the Catholic League and the Huguenot armies of Henry of Navarre. These were virtually local conflicts, but the area had its share in most Continental or global affairs.

Tulle has had a long and bloody history. It was taken and retaken by the English during the Hundred Years War, each successful assault being followed by a massacre. In the 13th century, the Lord-Abbot of Tulle, Elie of Ventadour, set his flock a very poor example when, finding the abbey coffers somewhat empty, he borrowed large sums from the local Jews, offering a high rate of interest. Then, in his secular judicial capacity, he accused them of usury, and had them condemned to death.

During the Wars of Religion, in the 16th century, the town was again sacked in turn by the Huguenots and the Catholic league. The great Turenne himself led the Protestant army against the town.

History does repeat itself, even in tragic form, and it struck again in the late World War. The Maquis of Corréze rose against the Germans and liberated the town just after D-Day in 1944. S.S. troops re-took the town a few days later, and hanged eighty of the inhabitants from the lamp-posts along the main street.

However, to strike a happier note, not far from Tulle, on a steep hill, lie the ruins of a castle, and here, some time around 1140, Bernard of Ventadour was born. He was a troubadour, perhaps the greatest of them, and if you reflect that without the troubadours much of our poetic heritage from medieval Europe would either have been lost or never existed, his name deserves to be remembered.

According to his biographer, Uc de St-Cire, "*he was handsome and adroit, could sing and make verses and was well informed and courteous.*"

The Count of Ventadour grew fond of him and so, unfortunately, did the Count's wife . . . "*so much that he made verses to her, and their love lasted a long time, and the Count knew it not . . .*" Ah-ha!

When the Count found out he chased Bernard from his castle,

but you can't keep a good troubadour down for long and he went to the Court of the Duchess of Normandy ... "*who was young and of great merit, and he was smitten by her, and her of him and he made many good songs.*"

Considering his humble origins (his father was the castle baker) and his ability to attract the wives of powerful and intelligent men, it is happy to recall that after a long and not uneventful life, Bernard died peacefully in a cloister.

He only composed forty-five poems, but he was among the first of the troubadours and we shall hear of them frequently in our travels, for they, like us, were wanderers, roaming from town to town and castle to castle, for whatever the wars, troubadours and *jongleurs* were always welcome, often travelling at will between rival armies.

The *jongleurs* pre-dated the troubadours, and apart from singing and playing, were also acrobats and performed tricks. The modern word 'juggler' is a corruption of jongleur, while the word troubadour comes from the old French '*trouvère*' which means *discoverer*, so, as you can see we have much in common.

*   *   *   *

From Tulle it is a short run to the start of this particular journey at Argentat, and Argentat is a pretty place, well worth a visit. The Auberge de Gabare, on the *quai* below the bridge is a pleasant spot from which to view the town and river, even in spate, and with an excellent lunch presently available for F.25 (£3), wine included, is a good place to fortify oneself for the coming journey, or rest for a day after the long drive south.

Besides this, Argentat is an interesting old town, full of fine buildings and with some interesting spots to visit in the country round about.

The Dordogne changes direction there, swinging west, and the upper river has been frequently dammed for hydro-electric power. The river is only navigable downstream, and then only by canoe. A tour up to the north will eventually take you to Serrièresle-Chateau, a little fortified town, with a fine castle and then, on an island in the river Marronne to the towers of the castles of Merle. I say castles, because the site illustrates the problems caused by the French custom of divided inheritance. In England, the eldest son got the lot, and his younger brothers had to rely on his goodwill. In France, the inheritance was shared, and while a large estate might have sufficient territory to absorb the entire brood, the sons of Merle refused to move from their birthplace, until by the end of the Hundred Years War, no less than seven septs of that warlike clan were crammed onto their ancestral island. It took another two hundred years and the cannon of Richelieu to blast them loose.

There is a fine view of their castles from the bridge above the town, or there would be, were the rain not sheeting down. But it was, so I put the camera away and turned south, for Figeac.

2

The Lot and the Celé

If you turn west, south of Argentat, and run alongside the Dordogne for some fifteen miles to Beaulieu, you arrive in Quercy, that ancient province which borders the *département* of the Dordogne, in the neighbouring province of Périgord. Crossing the little Cère, below Beaulieu, you enter the *département* of the Lot, and arrive instantly among a host of attractions, not least the continuation of the Dordogne itself. You will notice that most French *départements* are named after the principal local river.

The road runs past the castle of Castelnau, which apart from being a great fortress and the seat of a powerful baron was, in medieval times, held from its overlord on payment of a most unusual quit-rent.

Quit-rents are token payments for an estate, usually of a symbolic rather than a monetary nature, and were not uncommon in the Middle Ages — or even today, for that matter. The Knights of St. John, for example, held Malta from the King of Spain, and paid him an annual rent of a hawk. In England, the Dukes of Marlborough and Wellington still hold their estates from the Crown on the annual payment of a French guidon, to commemorate their ancestors' victories at Blenheim and Waterloo. What would happen if the present Dukes ever forget to hand it over doesn't bear thinking about, but in theory the estates revert to the Crown.

In 1184, the overlord of Castelnau, the Count of Toulouse, gave the lordship of the castle to his favourite, the Vicomte of Turenne, at which the baron of Castelnau instantly rebelled and appealed over the Count's head to the then King, Louis VIII. The quarrel was settled, after some bloodshed, on payment of an annual tribute; one egg. Every year the egg was conveyed from Castelnau to Turenne by a herald, accompanied by an armed escort! The quit-rent was paid until the late 16th century, and never once forgotten, until the Wars of Religion made such matters out of date. You can visit Castelnau, and although much restored, it remains a fine example of a medieval castle.

To the west of Castelnau lie two worthwhile visits, the first to the great caves and underground river at Padirac, and the other to the pilgrimage town of Rocamadour.

Rocamadour is a fantastic sight, clinging leechlike to a sheer cliff, and was at one time a stop on the road to Compostella and a pilgrimage centre in its own right, for it contains, in a small chapel, one of the rare 'Black' Virgins. Black Virgins are now very rare, and are more often found in the Auvergne. On the few occasions when one has been cleaned, they have been found to be gilded, the black caused by centuries of candle smoke, although some are quite literally black, brought so they say, from the East — perhaps looted from an Orthodox Byzantine church by a Crusader, or reproduced from some icon, where the Madonna is usually of a dusky, middle-eastern complexion.

The one at Rocamadour is very old, and a patron of soldiers and prisoners. Her chapel is hung with their fetters, glinting dully in the flickering light of the pilgrim candles. The shrine was looted in the 12th century by soldiers of Henry Fitzhenry, son of Henry II of England.

I could write at length about Rocamadour, which is one of my favourite places, but having already done so in my book on the Dordogne, we must pass it by and travel on to Montal.

* * * *

There is nothing the French like more than love, and love, mother's love anyway, is enshrined at the Château of Montal.

The Lot near Figeac

Jeanne d'Entraygues, widow of the Lord of Montal, loved above all, her eldest son Robert. In 1523 he rode off to serve his King, Francis I, in the Italian Wars, and in his absence his mother decided to build him a beautiful manor as a welcome-home present. No expense was spared and the construction was far advanced when the news came of the French defeat at Pavia. Rumour had it that Robert was taken prisoner and carried off to Madrid, but as the years passed no news of his fate reached his anxious mother at Montal. Eventually she realised that he had died in captivity and would never come home, so on the open gable-end her mason carved the sad epitaph '*Plus d'espoir*'. 'No more hope'.

Montal is a beautiful place and thankfully the history does brighten up considerably later on, thanks to a recent owner, Maurice Fenaille, who died here in 1937. Monsieur Fenaille was an oil millionaire and when he purchased Montal in the 1920s, the castle was an empty shell.

To Fenaille, Montal was more than a home, it was an obsession. He scoured the world and spent a fortune to restore Montal to its former glory. Not as a replica, or reproduction, but *exactly* as it was in its glory, with period furniture, paintings, tapestries and household goods. It stands renewed today, beautiful as ever, and if the pleasure it gives the eye is any yardstick, perhaps money can buy happiness after all.

*   *   *   *

Figeac, on the Celé, is a very old town. It stands in a valley at the eastern tip of the Causse de Gramat, and has acted for centuries like the cork in a bottle, plugging the routes on either side, always a fortress now a tourist centre and once, like Rocamadour, a stop on the road to Compostella. The pilgrims did not all follow one main road. No one town could have fed them, or given them shelter. They drifted across the country, some by one route, some by another, following a general course to the south-west.

In Figeac the old buildings in the town are somewhat decayed and only the Hotel de La Monnaie in the centre, where the King's taxes were collected, is really worth visiting, although a wander up the back streets to the church of Le Puy can be rewarding. The old buildings lean in until the roofs almost touch, shadowing the lanes below.

Figeac has two famous sons, the first of whom, the actor Charles Boyer, once had every lover in the world whispering "*Come wiz me to zee Casbah*" in the ear of his beloved, while the other, and possibly an even more romantic figure, was Jean-François Champollion.

"And who" you are saying, "is he?"

Champollion was the man who cracked the secret of the Rosetta Stone, and in so doing took archaeological knowledge forward (or backward) thousands of years. Champollion was born in Figeac in 1790. The son of a bookseller, he was a child prodigy, speaking several languages by his early teens and making a brilliant school and university career as a teacher and historian. He wrote his first book '*A History of Famous Dogs*' when he was only eleven.

When Napolean set off to invade Egypt in 1799 he took with him numerous savants and during the excavations one of them unearthed what is now the 'Rosetta' Stone, which was of course found at Rosetta in the Nile Valley.

The stone is a large piece of black basalt, inscribed with a religious decree passed by Egyptian priests about 200 B.C. The inscription is in three languages, each with its own section, the top in hieroglyphics, the second in demotic script, and the lowest in Greek. It was the same message, given in different languages.

Champollion was a Greek scholar, and he applied his knowledge of that language and some really inspired guesswork to decipher the other scripts. His real genius lay in realising that the enclosed figures, the 'cartouches', were representations of the Pharaohs, in this case Ptolemy. Thanks to his efforts, archaeologists today can now read the inscriptions of the Pharaohs, and the frontier of human knowledge expanded to embrace yet another ancient civilization.

Figeac, naturally enough, is very proud of Champollion, and in a square by the Church of St. Sauveur, a little version of Cleopatra's Needle is erected in his honour. Figeac would probably like to have the Rosetta Stone, but it was wrested, with some difficulty, from the baggage of a French general, and now occupies a prominent place in the Britsh Museum. Even Champollion had to work from a plaster replica.

*   *   *   *

Our travels from Figeac to Cahors take us to and fro between the valleys of two rivers, the Celé and the eastern Lot. This a wooded area with low hills criss-crossed by little valleys, each concealing a castle, a church, or a small village. This is a trip to linger over, and a good place to stay at is the *Hotel Les Frottes* in Calverets, a little west of Figeac. The Lot is by far the larger river, but the fast-flowing Celé, one of those rivers which waters a land 'where the tourists don't go', shelters some beautiful villages and some forgotten, yet interesting stories.

A little south of Figeac lies Capdenac, a hill town, once a

The Celé

Roman fortress, but now largely in ruins. It has a well-restored
Romanesque church, the vault of the nave so buttressed as to be
almost flat, and some splendid views over the river Lot itself.
Sully, Henry IV's minister, once lived here, within easy dash of
the Spanish frontier, should his master turn difficult.

West of Capdenac, by winding roads, lies Cahors, and we are
going to travel to and fro across the hills until we get there, stopping first of all at two villages, the Toiracs, St. Pierre and Larroque. The Lot itself is one of the great rivers of Southern France,
rising in the Cévennes and flowing eventually into the Garonne.
Like the smaller Aveyron, we shall meet it constantly in our travels, and hereabouts it is a wide, winding stream, usually rather
shallow in summer, but this year swollen by the late rains.

Saint-Pierre has a Romanesque church and apart from that, little to commend it, but Larroque has the ruins of a fine castle with
an enormous keep, now reduced in height but still an excellent

31

Ste Eululie sur Celé

example of the medieval fortress. The reader will realise by now that I prefer castles to churches and he would be right, but it is time to turn north again and head for the village of Espagnac-Ste-Eululie, on the Celé, in a smaller valley to the north of the Lot.

The Celé is a swift shallow river and in this part, between Capdenac and Espagnac, once went by the name '*Val Paradia*' Paradise Valley, and it is indeed very beautiful. The best view of Espagnac, which is a really gem-like little village, can be obtained from across the river, before you cross the little bridge into the village itself. Ste. Eululie is said to be the prettiest village in Quercy.

The village church with its charming wooden bell tower was once part of the Priory of the Val Paradis, re-built in the 15th century and, unusually for a French church, contains effigies of the local lords, dating from the 13th and 14th centuries. The village is quiet, deserted in the heat of the day, and quite lovely.

A little north of Espagnac, on the causse de Gramat, lies Assier, where the church has another magnificent tomb, this time of Galiot de Genouillac, Master of the Ordnance to Francis I, another attendant at the fatal field of Pavia, and buried here in conspicious military glory. The tympanum and tower of the church are decorated with warlike scenes, as are the remains of his château. It is the only church I have ever seen which instructs the visitor in siegecraft.

Marcilhac-sur-Celé, set in the valley, is yet another of those villages with an 'ac' ending. I understand, and have long believed, that the '*ac*' comes from the Roman *aqua*, water, but some authorities claim that the origins are older than that and means simply 'place'. You can take your pick. Either seems possible, for it would have been foolish to establish a village in any place without water.

The abbey at Marcilhac had a turbulent history. The monks once owned the sanctuary at Rocamadour, but since it had no value, and they had no need of it, they let it pass to the monks of Tulle. However when, after the discovery of the body of St. Armadour there the pilgrims started flocking to Rocamadour, they tried to get it back, and a long legal wrangle began. This lasted for years, progressing by appeal after appeal up to the Holy

33

See itself. The Pope finally awarded the shrine to Tulle, and 3,000 ducats as compensation to Marcilhac. The abbey is interesting because it contains both Romanesque and Gothic architecture in the one building. An added attraction is that on the three occasions I have visited it, the abbey has been completely deserted, quiet, dead, empty. One barred cell contains a life-size statue of St. James, his robe painted with the scallop shells of Compostella. There is a nice walk along the river, which takes you past the cells and around the walls. Crossing back to the Lot and St. Cirq-Lapopie is to find a very different place, but then St. Cirq is the picturesque hill-town that goes on all the postcards so that the village is usually crowded and humming with the noise of cars and people. The tourists are drawn there by the sight of the fortress of Lapopie, now in ruins but still spectacular. The church and castle are perched on the very edge of the cliff high above the river. Inside, the church itself is huge, cool, white-washed and empty, which enabled my companion to nip smartly up into the pulpit and deliver an impromptu sermon on the theme 'You must be good'!

St. Cirq is a medieval town with narrow cobbled streets, wide terraces, tubs and boxes of flowers and huddled houses, roofed with red tiles. It was once the fief of the Lords of Lapopie, who built the château in the 11th century and defied their overlords from it for the next four hundred years. Even the redoubtable Richard Coeur-de-Lion retired from these walls and he claimed, with some justification, that he could take any castle that he put his mind to. All around Lapopie is castle country and you can visit, within a few miles, those of Cénevières and Calvignac, or the château of Gontaut-Biron.

From St. Cirq-Lapopie the road runs, through tunnels in the rock, back again across country to the Celé, which is wider now, and we arrive at the village of Cabrerets, mainly drawn by the evocative name of the 'Castle of the Devil' there. Once actually on the ground the castle is hard to find. You will finally locate it, glued to the rock-face a little above the bridge, facing the village. Like many 'castles' it was constructed by fortifying a deep cave eroded in the rocks by wind and river. Such fortresses can be

Marcilhac, the Abbey

found all over this part of France, and there is a notable one in the Vezère valley in Dordogne. Many of these fortresses served to shelter prehistoric tribes and in some cases have been occupied for one reason or another, from remote times right up to the present day.

The 'devils' who once occupied it were, needless to say, English mercenaries, unemployed during the lulls in the Hundred Years

St Cirq-Lapopie

Streets of St Cirq

War, who preyed on the locals for a living until the wars broke out again.

The Celé finally joins the Lot a little below Cabrerets and we turn west again to the Grotto of Pech-Merle, another deep cave, decorated with mesolithic paintings and unlike the admittedly much finer ones at Lascaux, these can actually be visited. This part of the Lot is full of deep caves, many of which are open to the public, and contain prehistoric paintings or carvings. For the student of prehistory, Quercy is a treasure-house, but for less remote enthusiasms, let us press on down the valley, to the walls of Cahors.

3

Cahors and the Agenais

Cahors, capital of Quercy, is a fine attractive city. Even the name has a ring to it. The city pre-dates the Romans, who built the first bridge hereabouts and, like the Gauls, worshipped the goddess Divona, a water sprite who lived where the spring flows out of the rocks into a blue-green pool on the south bank of the river. This spring still supplies drinking water to the city, as it has done for over 2000 years.

The city stands on a wide sweep of the Lot, and was originally fortified by the building of a wall, parts of which still remain, across the neck of the isthmus. This sealed off the city from landward attack and the river completed the protective encirclement. Three bridges span the river today, the Pont-Neuf, the Pont Louis-Phillipe, and the famous Pont Valentré, and only the last is attractive.

The Pont Valentré is, deservedly, one of the sights of Europe, a fortified bridge dating from 1308, which still stands and carries traffic and has beauty, utility, and even legend, to add to its charm.

The story goes that the mason entrusted with the work soon realised that he would never complete the bridge on time without some supernatural assistance. He therefore made a pact with the Devil, in which the Devil was to assist in the work and, most important, obey all the orders of the architect. On the successful

Divona fountain, Cahors

completion of the work, the architect, for his part, would surrender his soul. All in all a fairly commercial sort of pact, and not one to enter into lightly.

Satan then turned-to with a will and the work proceeded so well that it soon neared completion, at which point, not surprisingly, the builder began to fear for his future. Various obstacles were put in the Devil's path, but all seemed up for the mason's soul, until he had a brainwave. The devil was ordered to fetch water for the workers — and handed a sieve. Somewhat put out at losing an architect, who are handy folk to have about, Satan went to the top of the central tower — still called the Tower of the Devil — and hurled down stones on the workforce. One can hardly blame him! The topmost stone still bears a carving of the devil attempting to dislodge it.

Legend apart, the bridge was the bastion of the town's defences. It still has three towers of the original five, and machicolated buttresses on the side walls. Cahors is surrounded with low hills, called locally '*peuchs*', and the towers on the bridge were built high enough to overlook the surrounding heights. The bridge was plastered during restoration in the last century, but most of this has now flaked off, leaving the bridge near enough as it was in the Middle Ages. Incidentially, '*peuchs*' are found all over this part of France, and many villages in Cantal are called Peuch-something-or-other. In every case they stand on a spur.

The land walls are also imposing, with a high keep or barbican by the river and beside the north road, the ominously named *Tour des Pendus*, the Tower of the Hanged, from which the suspended bodies of malefactors gave new arrivals a good idea of what would happen to anyone who fell foul of the local justice. The town belonged, for a while, to the Templars, and then was given to the local Bishop, who held secular as well as ecclesiastical control. At one time the trade of the town was controlled by merchant families from Lombardy, the commercial wizards of the Middle Ages. Lombard Street, in the banking area of London, is another mark of their success.

To remind the citizens of the Bishop's control, his helmet, sword and gauntlets were displayed on the altar during Mass, and any new Bishop was met at the Pont Valentré by the local citizens and nobility who, barefoot, were obliged to lead him to his Cathedral. As some compensation the nobles received all the silverware and dishes used at the Bishop's first banquet, and when one Bishop tried to wriggle out of this commitment, they smashed the dining room to pieces.

The English frequently besieged the town in the Hundred Years War, and Henry of Navarre took it by storm after an eight-day siege in 1580 during the Wars of Religion, but the town is not just a warlike relic. It is now an attractive market town, a wine and tourist centre, and the birthplace of some notable people. It had a university, founded in the 14th century by one of its sons, and a Pope, John XXII. Other natives include the poet Clement Marot (1495-1544), who translated the Psalms into Reformation

Pont Valentré, Cahors

The Tower of the Hanged, Cahors

anthems, was a trusted friend of Margaret of Angouleme, and also noted for his epigrams. Above all, there was Gambetta.

*   *   *   *

Leon Gambetta was born in Cahors in 1838, the son of an Italian grocer and a Frenchwoman from Gascony. As a boy he wanted to be a sailor and even when he became a successful lawyer, retained some nautical characteristics; his drinking was heavy, and his morals deplorable. By the time he was thirty, his bohemian private life left him decidedly dishevelled, with greying hair and an unkempt beard, but he was also — and on this rests his enduring fame — an advocate of distinction and a great orator.

To the French of the Second Empire, Gambetta had all the fire and passion of Danton, and when the Empire collapsed at the start of the Franco-Prussian War, and Paris was besieged, Gambetta became Minister of the Interior, and raised a militia of 300,000 men for the defence of the threatened capital.

The provisional Government of France was now established at Tours, where it was decided Gambetta should join them. On 17th October, 1870, he left Paris in a balloon, floated south across the German lines, and became Minister of War. Although France surrendered, Gambetta made an honourable defence, and the terms of the treaty were such that the occupying forces left France within the year, although they took with them much French money, all French pride, and the provinces of Alsace and Lorraine. While all this was going on the Paris commune rose in revolt, and was bloodily suppressed by Government troops. Gambetta had already resigned as War Minister and insisted that the surviving insurgents were well treated after the defeat of the commune. In 1889 he introduced a bill to amnesty the survivors of the massacres, deportations and trials which the suppression of the commune had involved, and not surprisingly this has made him enduringly popular with the Left.

Statue of Gambetta, Cahors

Every French town has at least one street named after him and here in his birthplace, the wide Boulevard Gambetta is flanked by an even wider square containing his statue. He deserves it.

Present day Cahors is a small town, of about twenty thousand inhabitants, centre of a wine district and a stop for tourists on the road to Spain and Languedoc. It caters for them with some excellent restaurants, including the notable *La Taverne*, and some good hotels such as *Le Melchoir*, near the station.

The Syndicate has prepared a guide to the town, which if followed will take the visitor to all the sights including the Cathedral of St. Etienne. This has three Byzantine *coupoules* and a very beautiful cloister, although most of the statues have been defaced or wrenched from their niches by some vandal or other. Within the church, the choir is guarded by eight gilt angels and still retains traces of medieval frescoes.

The streets around St. Etienne are the oldest, and to my mind, the finest in the town, with many Renaissance buildings and courtyards, while out in the *quais* which run beside the Lot, the plane trees have been trained over the road to give shelter from the fierce southern sun.

Around Cahors lie the vineyards of the famous — if forgotten — black wine of Cahors, a rich dark red vintage, with a long and intriguing history, and still the most important industry of the town.

The Cathedral of St Etienne, Cahors

Caves at Parnac, Cahors.

Écoute le cri des vendages,
Qui monte du pressoir voisin,
Vois les sentiers rocheux des granges,
Rouges par les sang de raisin.

Cahors wine is darker than that of Lamartine's native Mâcon, and more sturdy than most red wines, and well merits the AC standard that it bears today. The Romans admired it and it was, so they say, the 'black wine' that drew the English into Quercy. Until the Revolution there in 1917, Cahors wine was especially popular in Russia, where it was served as Communion wine by the Orthodox Church. With the Russian Revolution of 1917, the great market for Cahors wine collapsed and is only now making a recovery. No effort is spared to tempt the visitor into trying and buying the local wine, and there is a well marked *Route du Vin* to lead the enthusiast out across the vineyards.

Over half the vintage is pressed in one co-operative, *Les Caves*

45

d'Olt, at Parnac. Other excellent growths come from Jouffreau, Tesseydre and Luzech.

Cahors, as we have noted, is the capital of Quercy, a province which runs almost from the edges of the Massif-Central in the north, south to the Garonne, and from Figeac in the east to the Agenais. Below Cahors lies the so-called Quercy-Blanc, which takes its name from the chalky rocks in the sub-strata which whiten the soil and lighten the landscape with a series of escarpments.

Quercy is pastoral country with sheep flocks wandering on the causses and the slopes of the rolling hills. Stunted oaks choke the open causse country where the nut-like truffles grow among their roots, to be sniffed out in winter by truffle hounds or a questing pig. Each small farmhouse, built of yellow stone and roofed with red tiles, contains a dove-côte somewhere in the fields or farmyard, each one full of fluttering pigeons. I had imagined that the birds were for eating, but when I asked about this, it was met with exclamations of horror! The birds provide essential manure and every bird is cherished. The idea of eating them seems quite repugnant, and indeed no local restaurant has them on the menu. Some of the dove-côtes are very large and many are quite beautiful. A dove-côte is, to my mind, the mark of Quercy. Other regions have them but not in such number or variety.

Our part of Quercy for this chapter, lies between the valley of the Lot and that of the Aveyron, which border the area, north and south respectively, and it runs out west into the fruit country of the Agenais.

To tour this area, take the road which leads out across the Pont Valentré and along the Lot to tiny Pradines, where the trip stops abruptly at the little restaurant, *'du Clos Grand'*, which is not only good and full of character, but full too, especially at lunchtime, with local people, which is always a good sign. If you want to eat there you will have to book ahead. This is a local restaurant, not a tourist trap.

The food in Quercy is good, but somewhat fattening. Lunch at the *du Clos Grand*, for example, commenced with a bread and potato soup, proceeded through an *omlette des cépes* and a steak,

46

A Dovecôte in Quercy

du Clos Grand, Pradines

to fruit, local *cabécous,* or goat cheese, and coffee. All this, except the coffee, is local fare and excellent, especially with *vin de Cahors.*

Living locally is, to my mind, the best, if not the only way to know France. In the Dordogne, for example, many English people have purchased 'homes' and settled down, but the great snag with buying a home abroad is that even if you don't live there you feel obliged to go there, to the same place, every year, which in a land as large and diverse as France would be a considerable limitation. Far better perhaps, to hire a holiday home somewhere different every time, and in France holiday homes of all sizes can be easily hired by renting a 'gîte'.

A gîte is, literally, a shelter, but in the holiday sense it can be a flat, a cottage, a little house, even half a château. They can be rented at moderate cost, through the local *Syndicate d'Initiative,* in most parts of rural France. The *département* of the Lot, for

A gîte near Cahors

example, has currently some 250 gîtes for hire. The basic idea is that apart from supplementing the number of available hotel rooms, which are never too plentiful in rural areas, it provides the locals with some badly needed extra income. Apart from the rent itself, they also earn money by providing local produce, cheese, milk from the cow, eggs, and fruit from the trees. I stayed at one near Arcambal and another near Rodez. Both were good, excellent value, and the gîtes have gained another convert. I recommend them to you as an excellent way of seeing France and meeting the French.

*   *   *   *

The road west to the Agenais leaves Cahors by the Pont Valentré, and follows first the south bank, giving fine views over the river to the north, especially of the château at Mercues, now an excellent, if expensive hotel overlooking the river. The road then takes you to Luzech. Not far away is a Gallic '*oppidum*' or hill fort, which gives some alternative views over the south bank, while Luzech itself, although little more than a village, is a lovely little place and well worth a lunch-time stop.

Puy-l'Eveque, the next stop was, as you may guess, once a possession of the Bishop of Cahors, who owned much of the land hereabouts, and it marked the most western outpost of the Bishop's domaine. The town was fortified and the ruins of the Bishop's castle can still be visited. If, however, you like castles, then a treat is shortly in store. Head northwest for Puy-l'Eveque and you will arrive at the great fortress of Bonaguil.

The Château at Bonaguil

The castle lies at the head of a valley, overlooked on many sides, and if you arrive in the late afternoon, from the south the château glows in the evening light. The castle has been recently and well restored, so that the *Café des Ruines* by the lower wall, is now none too aptly named, but if you leave your car here and go past the pond up to the donjon, you will see that the castle, whatever its present repair, was once a great garrison.

Although Bonaguil was started in the 13th century, much of what remains dates back to the mid-15th century and the construction, therefore, reflects the existence of artillery. There are bombard platforms within the castle and although overlooked by surrounding hills, all would have been out of range for the cannon of the late Middle Ages.

However, directly or indirectly, artillery made the medieval castle obsolete and after the Wars of Religion it fell into ruin and was neglected by various owners. It once changed hands for as little as a hundred francs and a bag of walnuts, which considering that the central keep, or Great Tower, was one of the largest fortifications in France, must have been something of a bargain, if only for the value in dressed stone.

After the expulsion of the English in 1453, Bongaguil became the home of the Baron of Blanquefort, Berenger de Roquefeul, "*who feared not man, God, or Devil*". He ravaged the countryside round about, hanging anyone who hesitated to comply with his demands and retreating to his fortress at Bonaguil when the outraged peasantry finally rose against him.

The castle is now open from Easter to October, and set as it is in this beautiful valley, is well worth a visit.

* * * *

From Bonaguil we go south through Fumel to Penne, our first stop in the Agenais.

The Agenais country extends from Quercy to the borders of Armagnac. It is a rich, fertile region, particularly devoted to fruit growing, especially plums, usually dried into prunes, and for the *jus des pruneaux*. This, the local firewater, is an agreeable drink, available in most shops and in every bar. Penne d'Agenais once belonged to Richard Coeur-de-Lion, and perched high up over the valley, is a natural strong point, built to serve as an outpost for the garrisons of Aquitaine.

From the road by Penne you will see on your left the somewhat Byzantine outline of the pilgrim church at Notre Dame de Peyragude. This is a modern building but built on the site of an ancient martyrdom, carried out, apparently, at the hand of the English; or so the locals say. I asked an old lady in Penne if she could tell me anything about that strange building on the hill and she said that it was "where they put them down the well".

"Who?"

"The English, of course."

"The English were put down the well?"

"NO, NO, Monsieur, the *English* put the people down the well. They did a lot of that, the English," she added darkly.

The atrocity was in fact carried out by Spanish mercenaries of the Catholic League in 1570, but the 'time of the English', gets the blame for most of the terrors in local history. Sidney's sentiment on *that sweete enemie, France,* was not reciprocated.

Villeneuve sur Lot, was a bastide, founded in 1253 by that great builder Alphonse de Poitiers. A great architect was lost to the world when Alphonse went off with St. Louis, his brother, to the Crusades.

He built many of the bastides in southern France, and although their original purpose was to resist the encroaching English, who were ever seeking wells to put people down, his little towns were, and still are very beautiful. In the course of this book we shall visit a lot of them and nearly all have great charm. Villeneuve is much bigger than most and still has many traces of the old fortifications, including the gateways, one of which, La Porte de Puyols, we go through on our way to Agen twenty miles away to the south. Before you do though, visit the little pilgrim chapel of Notre-Dame de la Bonne Encountre, perched precariously over the Pont-Vieux. The chapel was built by the English in the 13th century, no doubt taking a much needed break from stuffing the locals down wells!

The Chapel of La Bonne Encountre, Villeneuve-sur-Lot

Agen lies on the Garonne and is a market town of some size. In the late 16th century it was the home of Bernard Palissy who discovered the art of glazing pottery. At one crucial moment in his experiments he tried throwing his own furniture into the furnace to keep the fire going, which may have delighted his customers but certainly infuriated his wife.

Agen is also a staging point on the Canal-Lateral-a-la-Garonne, one of the great French canals and one that we shall meet again and again in this region. At Agen the canal strides out of the town over a great aquaduct with 32 spans, leading it away to the west, but we have reached our western limit and must turn back again towards Cahors and the Causse de Limogne.

> *"Across the valleys and the high land,*
> *With all the world on either hand,*
> *Drinking when I had a mind to,*
> *Singing when I felt inclined to ...*

... until the green waters of the Divona fountain diverted my path once again across the Pont Valentré.

4

Quercy and the Causse de Limogne

Labouchere once remarked that the French have the idea that wherever you go, even to the top of Mont Blanc, you are sure to find an Englishman there, reading a newspaper. Perhaps this explains why, even in the most remote causse, no one seems very surprised to see you.

A *causse* is a plateau. The causse de Limogne though, is not typical either of the Great Causses which we shall meet later around Millau, or even of its near neighbours, the 'Causses Mineurs', the 'Causse de Gramat' and the 'Causse de Martel', which lie immediately to the north and north-west of Cahors.

The causse de Limogne is greener, has many more flowers and trees and is, on a scorching summer day, an altogether more pleasant place to visit. The causse is also thickly planted with scrub oaks, little stunted trees which produce the black gold of Quercy, the truffle. Truffles normally flourish in the wintertime when they are sought out by carefully trained truffle-hounds, or excavated by the questing snout of a pig. They are, of course, the essential ingredient of Périgord cooking, itself one of the richest cuisines in France and much of this renown owes its due to the produce of the causse de Limogne, although Limogne lies in Quercy, the next province. Moreover, although it is not really a typical causse, this causse will serve as an excellent introduction to causse country in general, and Limogne has a few unique features of its own besides being a very interesting part of the historic province of Quercy.

Quercy lies to the south-east of Périgord, and is roughly divided into two parts, the High and the Low. The causse country lies in the Low part, and is, to my mind, the more attractive. The province once belonged to the Counts of Toulouse, and later passed into the hands of the powerful Dukes of Aquitaine. When Eleanor of Aquitaine married Henry II of England, Quercy was part of her dowry. The province was confiscated by the French in 1228 but returned to Henry III by St. Louis in 1259. During the Hundred Years War it was held by the English, and ravaged by the French when they finally ended the Plantagenet power in 1453.

Quercy is a land of windmills, and pigeon-côtes, of open spaces and discreet river valleys, of fine food and sparse habitation, and by touring the little causse de Limogne, you can get a fair sample of the entire province.

Limogne, the little town which gives its name to the causse, lies to the west of Cahors on the road to Villefranche-de-Rouergue. The causse itself lies mostly to the south of this road and runs well into Bas-Quercy, or Lower Quercy, or Quercy-Blanc. This is a region of low trees with wild flowers in profusion, full of sheep flocks with only scattered farmsteads where each building is roofed in flat slates and clings solidly to the soil, each with its pigeon-loft or windmill. Lonely or not, it is good travelling country, and following our practice of taking minor roads whenever possible, the best way out of Cahors is the road that leads to Lalbenque. This road passes through Anjols where the village pond, apart from supporting a veritable fleet of ducks, is surrounded by tilted washing-stones, bowed by generations of pounded linen.

Flower lovers will adore the causse. Yellow daisies are the backdrop to a wide range of plants and orchids. The causse country is everywhere a paradise of flowers which, considering the relative sparseness of the earth seems rather surprising. A walk across the causse reveals a great variety of flowers and it must be remembered that the underlying strata, as well as the earth cover, varies considerably. Foxgloves, campanula, and wild chicory bloom

56

On the Causse de Limogne

along the roadsides, while poppies, génet and asphodel are draped across the yellow rocks on the open plateau. In June the walls along the route are draped with honeysuckle and the scent in the evening is glorious.

Lalbenque is a great truffle centre and lies in the middle of numerous footpath routes on the *Sentiers des Grande Randonnée*. The *Sentiers* are, in short, footpaths, and in France as in England, there are groups of ramblers busily engaged in opening up the paths after generations of neglect, and way-marking them for others to follow. The great route to Compostella, GR65, from Le Puy to Toulouse, is itself a *sentier* for much of the way and is still easy to follow, for apart from the red and white waymarks, the boots of the medieval pilgrims have left a lasting trace. The old track is a depression in the hills. grooved by footsteps, much as the steps in old churches are worn away by congregations over the centuries.

57

Compostella Cross on the Causse de Limogne

From Lelbenque go east towards Bach and then north to Concots. This route is quiet and attractive, the countryside tinkling with sheep bells and studded with crosses, while in Concots a good lunch can be obtained at the *Hotel des Voyageurs*.

*   *   *   *

Limogne must have been a trade centre in prehistoric times for the countryside round about is full of dolmens and standing stones. I have a friend who believes, half-seriously, that dolmens were really prehistoric tents and that a circle of dolmens is no more than just a Stone-Age campsite. Certainly we have slept in them from time to time and they do make excellent tents, well drained and windproof. He may be right!

Like Lalbenque, Limogne is a truffle centre, and today it is only the truffle that keeps the little town alive.

Martiel, further east, has even more stone circles than

Dolmen, Causse de Limogne

Abbey of Loc-Dieu

Limogne, which can only be reached with considerable difficulty as they lie in the middle of thick woods, and it is at Martiel that we turn south for the great abbey at Loc-Dieu.

The abbey looks decidedly un-churchlike. It resembles a fortress which, in fact, it was until the 15th century, when it was acquired by the Cistercians as a defensive mission church. It was very necessary, in those jarring days to protect even the most pacific community from roving freebooters and the abbey is, therefore, remarkably well preserved. The abbey church predates the castle and is a fine example of the Cistercian style, plain, undecorated and with classic lines.

The road west to Caylus gives the traveller a sudden magnificent view of the town itself, seen from the opposite hill. Caylus is a classic little town, a *bastide*, with the usual cornieres and market hall. The hall itself is especially interesting, not only because of its size (and it really is immense) but because it still contains the ancient grain measure, the mark of a reputable market. This consists of a basin cut into a stone counter, with a hole drilled in the

60

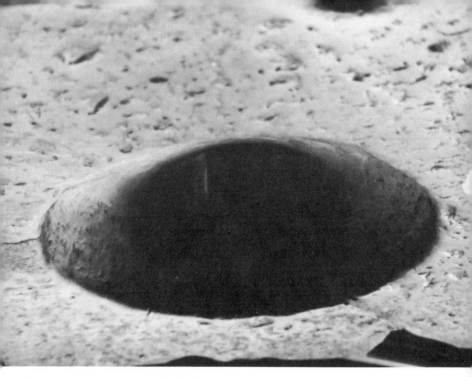

The grain-measure, market-hall, Caylus

bottom. The basin could contain a bushel of grain when filled to the brim, and the quantity thus agreed by buyer and seller, the stopper was removed and the grain then released into the purchaser's basket. All transactions took place in the public eye and short measure and other disputes were effectively thwarted.

A little stroll round Caylus is well worthwhile for it contains some curious houses. If you walk down to the church, you will see inside an impressive Christ carved by the Polish sculptor Zadkine in 1954. Zadkine's work has been affected by the Cubist School and this work in particular is striking, and not to be missed.

Opposite the 15th-century church stands the curious *House of the Wolf* which was built about 1250 and even today is decidedly creepy. What it must have looked like in former times, lit, if at all, by thin moonlight or flickering torches, is a blood-curdling thought. The house probably belonged to a huntsman and the

61

façade is decorated with wolf heads and the carvings of other wild animals, hunted, no doubt, on the wide slopes of the causse de Limogne.

The site at Caylus was inhabited in Roman times, for it is a natural fortress. In 1176 the Sieur de Montpezat obtained possession of the castle from the Count of Toulouse, only to lose it as a result of the Albigensian Crusade. It was rebuilt as a bastide ,by Alphonse de Poitiers in about 1270 and was then the strongest fortress town in Quercy, which did not prevent it falling to the redoubtable English knight, John Chandos, in 1362. The ramparts were demolished in the 18th century.

From Caylus you should try and visit the little 14th-century church at Notre-Dame de Livron nearby, for here at last (and at least) they once had a dragon! A knight-errant slew the dragon and built the little church to celebrate his victory and in gratitude to the angels who assisted him in combat. The church became a pilgrimage chapel and was still attracting pilgrims in the 17th century.

Lacapelle-Livron, nearby, is a Commanderie. It was built to protect the Livron pilgrims by the Order of the Temple in 1228 and passed to the Knights Hospitaller in the early years of the next century.

Pierre d'Aubusson, Prior of the Langue d'Auvergne, lived here after the Knights were expelled from their home on Rhodes and, after his death in 1497, the Commanderie became a prison for Knights sentenced for some infringement of their Rule. The Livron area is full of little attractions and you should try and visit Loze, St. Géry and the château at Cornusson, to the south. Cornusson was rebuilt in the 16th century by the Bishop of Vabre, and is in a remarkable state of preservation, well worth a stop before moving on to the market town of Caussade.

*   *   *   *

Caussade is a market town, largely devoted to the manufacture and sale of hats. To be bareheaded in Caussade is a solecism. The town stands at a gap in the hills where the causse peters out into the plain of Quercy and the great road runs south to Toulouse.

House of the Wolf, Caylus

Caussade dates back to 968 AD and was the seat of a viscountcy. One viscount used the castle to contain his large collection of concubines and lived there happily for many years until, overcome with remorse, or exhaustion, he became a monk in the abbey at Moissac.

A later viscount, Rotier, led his forces to the support of his lord, trying to raise the siege of Toulouse by the Albigensian Crusaders in 1209, arriving before the walls, "*with banners displayed and trumpets sounding,*" and although they were defeated, the town stayed in the viscount's possession until the early 15th century. The English took the town in 1362 and in 1392 it fell to the Count of Armagnac. It was a Huguenot stronghold during the Wars of Religion and suffered from several *dragonnades*, which meant that regiments of troops were billeted on the townspeople in the period after the Revocation of the Edict of Nantes, and urged to put their boots on the table, chase the maids, and generally behave like brutal and licentious soldiers should.

Straw hats have been made in Caussade for over a hundred years and in that time have graced the heads of European royalty and such artists as Maurice Chevalier.

*   *   *   *

North-east from Caussade lies the town of Puylaroque, which is both beautiful and interesting. It is perched on a hill, overlooking the plain towards Caussade and the outcrops of the causse de Limogne, and belonged to the Lords of Montpezat. Their town, Montpezat-de-Quercy, a little to the west, must also be visited. The church at Puylaroque contains a good medieval treasure, including a statue of that obscure saint, St. Voile, and a Virgin and Child. The church is buttressed by a little chapel, Notre Dame de Grace, built in 1364 by the Bishop of Evreux.

The Lords of Montpezat, the De Prés, were churchmen not soldiers. Their most distinguished member, the Cardinal Pierre De Prés, was Vice-Chancellor of the Church, and mediated, or attempted to mediate a peace treaty between France and England at the start of the Hundred Years War.

In Montpezat the Cardinal established a little university, a college, for the clergy, and endowed it not only with adequate funds, but with fine treasure, some of which has survived the centuries and still remains. The college contains various objects d'art, including some beautiful medieval coverings and jewel boxes and above all, some wonderful tapestries.

One of these, which it is claimed dates from the 5th century, shows the life and death of Alexander, while another 15th-century work shows the Cycle of the Year, the sowing, the reaping and the planting. The great tapestry in the nave shows scenes from the life of the knightly saint, St. Martin, and he is shown, as always, dividing his cloak and wrestling with the Devil. The church also contains the effigy of the Cardinal-benefactor. Finally, heading north again, we can take a little look at Castelnau-Montratier, before running back across the flower-decked causse to the valley of the Lot and Cahors.

5

Moissac and Montauban

The Tarn finally flows into the Garonne a little west of the small town of Moissac, and in the triangle thus formed the province of Quercy edges up to the province of Gers. While making a change from the stark beauty of the Causse, this district has a quite different charm of its own.

To visit this area it is as well to stay in Moissac, either at the *Hotel Poste* or the rebuilt and elegant *Chapon-Fin*, which you will find in the main square. The *Chapon-Fin* has an excellent restaurant, parking is immediately to hand in the square, and the hotel itself stands a short distance from the abbey and offers some useful advice in the event of emergency — or at least the notice in my bedroom did! "In the event of Fire, the visitor, avoiding panic, is to walk down the corridor — and *warm* the chambermaid." *Quel sangfroid.*

The great magnet for visitors must be the Clunic Abbey of St. Pierre in Moissac. The cloisters and in particular the south door, have to be seen. It is always hard to keep a guide book from sliding into an account of endless churches and cathedrals and the only way out is to be highly selective in the ones you choose to visit and recommend, but any selection must include Moissac.

The abbey was founded by the Benedictines in the 7th century and was one of the first Benedictine foundations in France. It was then destroyed and rebuilt several times in the course of the wars, especially those following the Arab invasions of the 8th century which devastated this part of France, and only ended with the expulsion of the Saracens by Charles Martel. The abbey was re-founded in the 11th century by the Clunic Order and much of the decoration owes its line to that Burgundian connection.

It should be pointed out that all monasteries acted as hotels in the Middle Ages, and none more so that those of the Clunics. Indeed, many of their abbeys were built just to serve the interests of pilgrims, and most of those on the road to Compostella — like Moissac — are Clunic creations.

The abbey was pillaged by the English in the 14th century, sacked by the Huguenots in the 16th century and mutilated by the Revolutionaries in the 18th century. It narrowly escaped emasculation in the 19th century when it was discovered that a proposed rail link between the ports of Bordeaux and Sète would run directly through the cloisters, but this last desecration was fortunately prevented.

The abbey today consists of two parts, the church reached via the great south door, and the cloisters reached from a separate

Tympanum, Moissac

entrance on the western side of the church. The church is basically Romanesque, with much late-Gothic work from about 1450. The overall effect serves as a setting for the south door, which is quite startling.

Lord Clark has written that the sculptor of Moissac must have been *"an eccentric of the first order, a sort of Romanesque El Greco."* Whoever he was, his name is forgotten, but he was probably one of those craftsmen who, because of his skill, could travel from place to place, protected by the Church and free from the restrictions of the trade guilds. These men, the *freemasons*, were greatly envied by the townspeople, and regarded with some awe by the labourers who assisted them. The name at least, is still with us, and still carries a certain cachet.

The theme of the tympanum at Moissac is St. John's vision of the Apocalypse. Christ sits in majesty, surrounded not just by saints and angels, but by mythical beasts, fierce hawks and dragons, while at his feet, heads canted attentively upwards, sit 24 old men, each clutching a viol. The detail and the craftsmanship is amazing and combine in a manner that the Clunic Order seems to have mastered, in that we have a work of art which is huge in size, yet delicate in detail.

It is worth remembering that this sculpture, like those in most churches of medieval times, would have been plastered and painted in bright colours. The effect then must have been entirely dramatic and it is hardly less so today. With the abbey church of Vézelay and the porch at Autun, the south door of St. Pierre in Moissac has to be seen by any true lover of medieval France.

* * * *

In spite of the spoilations we have noted, the rest of St. Pierre is well worth inspecting. The monks were dispersed at the Revolution, but the church still attracts a considerable congregation, and is also used for music festivals and the cultural events. In niches around the nave, various treasures are still on display including a beautiful '*Flight into Egypt*' of the 15th century, and a fine Virgin of Pity from about 1470. After seeing these you can go

Cloisters, Moissac.

out again, and turn right for the cloisters. If you arrive at the cloister door about 8.30 a.m. and tug the bell firmly, two things will happen. The châtelaine will appear from a house behind you, and you will then have the cloisters to yourself. Since, on this trip, we are trying to avoid crowds, an early start is often necessary, and as the abbey is only a few steps from the hotels, you can easily see it before breakfast.

The cloisters at Moissac are another 'must'. They are large and in excellent repair, dating from the Clunic foundation of the 11th century. Each pillar is decorated in the Romanesque style and faced with various carvings of the saints or scenes from the Old or New Testaments, while the central lawn of the courtyard is dominated by an immense cedar of Lebanon.

You should also visit the Moissac museum, for this shows the growth and importance of the historic abbey during the Middle Ages, and how, like so many Clunic foundations, it existed to

St Simon, the Cloisters, Moissac

help pilgrims on the road to Compostella. The museum also has displays of Queryçois life in both town and country.

As towns go, Moissac *ville* isn't very large. The population is only about 12,000 people, but it maintains its population and position, thanks partly to the abbey which brings the tourists, and partly to its position as a riverine port on the Canal-Lateral-à-la-Garonne. An evening stroll along the quiet canal, among the swooping swallows, and inspecting the moored *peniches*, makes the perfect finish to the day, especially if it follows the excellent dinner they serve in that excellent restaurant, the *Moulin de Moissac*.

*   *   *   *

The hinterland of Moissac is given over to fruit cultivation and the growing of table grapes, especially the *chasselas-doré*. These are grown in vineyards and orchards all across the flat lands between Moissac and the hill town of Lafrançaise.

Lafrançaise is a little place, living from the sale of table grapes, but built on the bluff overlooking the Tarn, with fine views across the plain below, and with a beautiful iron staircase fronting the *marie*. If you descend the hill and head south you will soon come to the town of Castelsarrasin. There is some dispute over the name of this place. On the face of it, it must mean the Castle of the Saracens, and since the Saracens certainly crossed this country to burn Moissac and fight Charles Martel, it is at least possible that they built a camp or fortress here, but the locals are quite convinced that, whatever the origin of the name, it isn't that!

If possible, try and visit Castelsarrasin on a Thursday, for this is market day and Castelsarrasin has one of the largest weekly markets I have ever seen. Every street is lined with booths and stalls and you can quite literally buy anything from a house to a pin, or a loaf to a bull, not to mention flowers, clothes, cakes, fruit, cheese, wine and all sorts of household and garden equipment.

Castelsarrasin is not a large town, barely larger than little Moissac, but it has a long history. It was a staging post on the road

71

from Toulouse to Bordeaux in Roman times and was a prize possession of the Counts of Toulouse a good deal later. After the Albigensian Crusade it was held for a time by the Knights of St. John. Some say that they reconstructed the town in the Moorish style and it thus acquired its Arabic-sounding name from the sight of the architecture, which seems unlikely. The town became a sub-prefecture of the *département* of Tarn-et-Garonne when Napoleon rearranged the *départements* in 1808, and has remained an important market centre ever since.

Napoleon, who had many excellent ideas, wanted to keep local government linked to the people it was supposed to serve and he decreed that each sub-prefecture should be so situated that the most remote resident could get there and back on horseback *in one day*. This caused government planners considerable headaches for they had intended to create the *départements* and sub-prefectures simply by ruling lines across the map. The curious shape of many French départements and sub-départements today, owes its origin to Napoleon's original decree.

Castelsarrasin has two churches, St. Saveur built in 1524, and St. Jean which was built by the Order of St. John, also dating from the 16th century, at a time when the Order itself was in decline. Neither is very interesting, and you can leave Castelsarrasin and head across the Garonne on the winding cross-country road to Montauban.

*   *   *   *

You can, of course, go directly to Montauban. It is the largest town hereabouts and all roads lead there, but the flat plain of the Garonne to the south is unvisited by tourists and makes for a gentle passage. Besides, it enables you to enter Montauban from the south, which is by far the most attractive route and you can arrive there across the Pont-Vieux and stop at once to visit the Musée Ingres.

Jean Auguste Dominique Ingres was born in Montauban in 1780. His father was an ornamental sculptor and Ingres was steeped in an artistic environment from birth. At eleven he went to school in Toulouse and lived there for six years, during which time he studied art and music and became an accomplished violinist. At seventeen he went to Paris and studied under David, the most famous artist of his day. From 1801 to 1824 he lived in Italy, but he regularly visited his native city and in 1824 painted his masterpiece, '*The Vow of Louis XIII*' for the cathedral in Montauban. It is said to be a masterpiece by those who ought to know, but I find it a dreary work on rather a dreary subject, the dedication of France to the Virgin by Louis XIII.

The Musée Ingres is full of his work and also contains his collection of *object d'art* and the works of other painters, for this is not just a tribute to a local celebrity, but holds the artist's own collection of works of art which he bequeathed to his native town. Ingres was a fine portrait painter and painted excellent nudes. His '*Portrait of Madame Gense*' in Montauban is an especially fine work and the museum itself is a most attractive building. It was once the Bishop's Palace, built in 1664 on the site of a castle once the home of the Black Prince. The great hall of the Black Prince is all that remains of the castle, but the Bishop's Palace is intact and makes an excellent museum.

In one room, in a glass case, stands the famous '*violin d'Ingres*' one of the few instruments to put a phrase into the French language. If a Frenchman has a hobby or some casual occupation to while away his idle hours, he has a '*passetemps*' — a pastime, but if he is good at it and it could, perhaps, be a consuming passion, then this is his *violin d'Ingres*.

Ingres was an excellent violinist, and in his youth was frequently torn between art and music. Art won in the end, but the phrase will live on.

The Musée Ingres stands on the banks of the Tarn and if you leave the car there and walk into the town, you will have no great difficulty in discovering a number of delightful spots.

Montauban is an old town, described by Michelin as a *puissante bastide* and a strong town it must indeed have been. The Tarn here marks the boundary between Quercy and the county of Toulouse and it was one of these counts who founded Montauban in 1144, not, as was usual, to protect the French from the rapacious English, but to protect the people of the district from the robber knights of Quercy.

During the Wars of Religion, the town was firmly Huguenot — even Calvinistic — and continued to persecute the Catholic minority even after the Declaration of the Edict of Nantes. These persecutions provoked reprisals and in 1621 Louis XIII descended on the town with 20,000 men and the Royal Artillery Train. However, the town withstood their attack for three months; a peace was patched up and for a while anyway, the Catholic forces withdrew. Seven years later, after the fall of La Rochelle had left Montauban as the last Protestant stronghold in France, Cardinal Richelieu, that warlike cleric, led the King's Army, and this time the townspeople opened their gates without a struggle. Richelieu destroyed the city walls and, although the outline can still be traced by following the line of the encircling boulevards which begin at the Jardin des Plantes, very little of the fortifications now remains.

Across the road from the Musée Ingres you can see the 'Dying Centaur' bronze to the war dead of 1914, by another local artist, Bourdelle, a pupil of Rodin. His work is well worth inspection and there is more of it in the Musée Ingres and, if you have the chance, still more at the Musée Bourdelle in Paris.

Although the walls have gone, there are still some military reminders and, overlooking the town stands the tower of the church of St. Jacques, which dates from 1230. This church, which was built for defence as well as worship, as are most 'bastide' churches, withstood various sieges and you can still see, on the walls, the marks of musket and cannon balls from the siege of 1621.

It also bears the inevitable *coquille* of its patron and is now being restored. The cost of the original church was met by fines imposed on the ladies of Montauban by the ecclesiastical court for breaking the laws against extravagant dress. One lady, who must have been wearing the very latest creation, was fined 1,000 tiles! It's an idea the present restorers might copy. A tax on bluejeans would make a fortune!

Across the road from St. Jacques lies the Museum of Pre-history and Natural History. This is well worth a visit, for apart from an enormous collection of stuffed animals from many continents, including over 2,000 exotic birds, it also has much useful information on the natural history and pre-history of Quercy.

Finally, before leaving this part of the town for a stroll round the streets, cast an eye at the Vieux Pont. It was built, entirely in brick, about the year 1305, on the orders of the French King, Phillip the Handsome. It is over 600 feet long and stands high above the river. Until the late 16th century it was fortified, like the Pont Valentré in Cahors.

Away from the river, take the road past St. Jacques, and a few steps will bring you into that lovely little square, the pride of Montauban, the *Place National*. Its presence completes the last essential feature of all *bastides*, the market square. This one, originally in wood, was destroyed by fire and rebuilt in 1649, entirely in brick. It is a delightful spot. Shops and cafes snuggle under the arches and the centre is occupied by a flower market until midday, so that at mid-morning you can take your coffee in the heavy scent of flowers.

The *Place National* stands in the old quarter of the town and if you wander off in any direction from there you will see many fine buildings and find at least one excellent hotel, the Hotel du Midi, where you would be well advised to have dinner.

The Cathedral of Notre-Dame, which stands near the Hotel du Midi, is a huge building, built in the classic style and dominated by immense statues along the pediments over the west door. Some of the giant figures have been moved inside the nave and it can't be said that they do a great deal for it. The church also contains *that* work by Ingres, '*The Vow of Louis XIII*'.

I suppose that as a pupil of David, who was himself much given to painting on such historic themes as the '*Oath of the Horatii*', which set Revolutionary Paris on its ear, it was inevitable that Ingres should try his hand at the same sort of thing, and the painting is regarded as a true work of art.

I've tried to like it, but I think it dull and I only labour the point because much of Ingres' work, especially his portraits, is delightful. It is perhaps no coincidence that this example of his work is

The Aveyron

kept here in the Notre-Dame, well away from the pleasures and treasures in the museum by the bridge. One last treasure in the town is the huge dove-côte in the grounds of the hospital on the road out to Moissac, still complete with coo-ing doves.

*   *   *   *

If you stay at the *Chapon-Fin* in Moissac, yet approach Montauban from Castelsarrasin and Montech, you could leave on the road that runs along the Tarn up to Villemade. Just above here lies the confluence of the Tarn and the Aveyron, and a little circuit along the Aveyron up to Negrepelisse rounds off our visit to this region. Negrepelisse stands on the edge of Rouergue and there, with the flat plain of the Tarn at our backs and the gorges of the Aveyron before us, let us stop.

Negrepelisse is a little place, named from the fact that it was once a centre for the charcoal-burners who worked in the nearby forests. The name is a corruption of *Noire Fourrure*. The bell tower of the brick-built 15th-century church is worth nothing, firstly because we shall from now on see a great many brick-built buildings, and because the bell tower is the *type-toulousain*, pierced by slots to let the clamour out. You will find bell towers of this type all over the hinterland of Toulouse and they are as typical of that region as the dove-côtes are of Quercy. We are on the very edge of Quercy, which belonged to the English, and we press on south now into the county of Toulouse.

6

Toulouse

Toulouse, the Red City — 'in more ways than one'. My guide, in pointing out how much of the city was built in rose-hued brick, was making a shrewd observation. It is curious how some places have a continuing strain running through their history. A warlike past is often due to geography, or the presence of a frontier, while commerce often evolves from some strategic advantage as a result of a ford or bridge, but some strains are more subtle. Toulouse, though, has always been a politically active place, with a strain of intolerance and revolution, while for the last half-century anyway, it has been a bastion for the Left. Given that urban France has usually leaned towards socialism anyway, this inclination in Toulouse received a large jolt in 1939 following the defeat of Republican Spain, and with the influx of Catalan refugees. The frontier is not far away and, hope springing eternal, many Spaniards settled in Toulouse and soon became involved in local politics. All this, and the large university, is by way of explaining why the walls of Toulouse are more slogan-daubed than in any other city I have visited. The spray-can might have been invented for the bourgeois revolutionary, so much use have they made of it. Apart from the odd demonstration, it seems to go no further, for as my guide pointed out, inside most revolutionaries lurks the *petit bourgeois*. But, this apart, what of Toulouse?

It is very large, the fourth city of France, with a population of

The Garonne at Toulouse

nearly half a million and is the ancient capital of Languedoc, and of the present region of Midi-Pyrenees. It is a very old town with a turbulent history and several curious stories, all well worth relating.

Toulouse stands in the valley of the River Garonne, lying on both banks of the river, and is a riverine port for the Canal du Midi, which flows south-east towards the Mediterranean, and its westward continuation, the Canal-Lateral de Garonne. It stands also at the western end of that great valley that swings up from the Mediterranean between the Pyrénées, and the southern outcrops of the Cévennes, past Carcassonne and Castelnaudry, before spreading out into the plains of Gascony.

The Visigoths founded Toulouse, and made the city their capital for a while before the Teutonic Franks crossed the Loire and drove the Goths across the Pyrénées and into Spain. In the 8th century, the Saracens swept in from Africa, destroying the city and ravaging the countryside as far as Moissac before marching north to their defeat at the hands of Charles Martel, near Poitiers.

Under the reign of the early Capets, Toulouse became a possession of those great lords, the Counts of Toulouse, one of the three great seigneurs of 12th- and 13th-century France, the others being the Dukes of Aquitaine and Normandy, who were also from time to time the Kings of England. The Counts spent a great deal of energy warring with Aquitaine, and in avoiding too much interference by the King, until the county was overwhelmed by the cataclysmic Albigensian Crusade.

Raymond de St. Gilles, Count of Toulouse, had been one of the leaders of the First Crusade which, at the end of the 11th century, re-took Jerusalem from the Moslems. His descendants, two generations later, embraced and supported the faith of the 'heretical' Albigensians and thus provided the then king of France, Louis VIII, with the means to extirpate their house.

The Albigensians, or Cathars, as they were more generally known, preached a version of the heretical Arian heresy, and having resisted conversion at the hands of St. Dominic, were out-

The Capitole, Toulouse

Execution site, Capitole, Toulouse

lawed by the Church and subjected to a terrible revenge. The Pope declared a Crusade against them and Louis VIII of France used the Crusade to destroy the Counts and absorb their land into the French demesne. The Crusaders were led by one Simon de Montfort, grandfather of that other Simon who founded the English Parliament and was killed at Evesham. The crusading Simon, having sacked Béziers and massacred the inhabitants, then took Carcassone and murdered the young Viscount. Simon was himself killed by a stone from a mangonel while besieging Toulouse.

The town suffered no more nor less than most French towns during the Hundred Years War, and the Wars of Religion, and only rose to military prominence again in 1814 when the soldiers of Wellington's Peninsular Army fought the penultimate battle of the Napoleonic Wars outside the city. Although no one knew it, Napoleon had abdicated four days previously, but news of this event had not yet reached the south, so the battle went on anyway. The scars of musket and cannon balls can still be seen on old buildings in the town around the Place de Capitole. The Revolution marked the town as a political centre, for it was a group of men from Toulouse and the river valley who formed the deputation from the Gironde which played a leading part in running France during the early years of the Revolution, and became known as the Girondin party.

The history of Toulouse has been turbulent, and through it all like an under-lying theme, lies a strong thread of intolerance. Bullet scars and spray-can slogans tell a truer picture than their perpetrators might imagine.

*   *   *   *

To see Toulouse it is best to drive directly into the centre and park as close as possible to the Place de Capitole and walk from there. Parking is a nightmare in any large town and it is best to abandon the car as soon as possible.

Most of the sights of the town are within easy reach and there are scores of hotels of all prices and standards within a short walk.

The Capitole itself, now the *Hotel de Ville*, is an imposing building with an 18th-century façade, fronting a building of medieval origin, itself rebuilt in the late 16th century. In the inner courtyard the visitor is confronted by a fine bronze statue of Henri IV in a huge niche, while on the ground a plaque records that this is the execution site where Henri, Duke of Montmorency, lost his head in 1631. Henri was one of a number of earnest, well-meaning lords, led into mischief by that unsavoury character '*Monsieur*' Gaston, Duke of Orleans, brother of Louis XIII. Plots against Richelieu, Louis' great Chancellor, were constantly being organized by '*Monsieur*', and just as constantly discovered. Kinship kept the King from executing his brother, but his dupes were not so lucky. The excuse for rebellion was always the same, "*to free the King from the influence of his advisers*", that is, Richelieu. Montmorency was Governor of Languedoc when he rebelled

Eglise du Taur

in 1630. He was quickly defeated and captured at Castelnaudry and executed at Toulouse. '*Monsieur*' escaped scot-free, as usual, and went on to plot yet again with the equally unsavoury, and equally unfortunate, Cinq-Mars.

The original Capitole housed the *Capitouls*, or Consuls, who governed the city for the Counts, and later for their various successors. Several French towns were run by Consuls, a practice which usually indicates a Roman or Visigothic origin in the town's constitution. It was also the seat of the *Parlements* of Toulouse, one of the several provincial *Parlements* in France, which functioned up to the Revolution.

From the Capitole there are interesting attractions on every hand. First head down the Rue du Taur, towards the huge bulk of St. Sernin, but stopping after a few metres at the Eglise du Taur with its stupendous steep brick façade. St. Sernin had suffered martyrdom on this spot in about 250 AD, being savaged to death by a bull and until the Reformation the church itself was called St. Sernin du Taur.

A fresco above the altar depicts the martyrdom, and the

St Sernin, Toulouse

church, a vast gloomy place, was once a fortified strongpoint standing as part of the town walls.

The Romanesque church of St. Sernin, further down the street, looks at first sight a shabby disappointing place. It is the largest Romanesque church in Western Europe and looks it. Built of brick and stone into an imposing pile, once inside it is revealed as a beautiful building, the pale rose brick on the walls glowing in the light, and containing many interesting relics. It is a pilgrim church in its own right, and a stop on the route to Compostella.

If you enter by the south door, the Porte Miégeville, you will see that of the two flanking statues, one is St. Peter with his keys, while the other inevitably, is St. Jacques. The first church of St. Sernin was commenced in about 400 AD to shelter the relics of St. Sernin and later endowed with numerous other relics by Charlemagne. The present church contains relics of 128 saints including the bodies of six apostles, plus such treasures as a thorn from the 'Crown of Thorns', a piece of the True Cross, and various other religious items and objects of veneration, as well as the sepulchres of three of the Counts of Toulouse. The saints are well represented and there is a fine statue of St. Roch, shown as usual with his dog and ulcerated thigh, but dressed here as a Compostella pilgrim, and another to my favourite saint, St. Jude, who is the patron saint of hopeless causes! Significantly, a great many candles were burning before his altar.

The present St. Sernin, rebuilt to cope with the influx of pilgrims, was started in 1080 and took 250 years to complete. It is a mixture of brick and stone and although the exterior is in urgent need of repointing, the inside has been cleaned and it is a fine and interesting church. The Place St. Sernin is the site of a large weekly market, held on Sundays between 8 a.m. and 1 p.m. where you can buy practically anything from a suit of clothes to a midday meal.

If you leave St. Sernin and pass the Musée St. Raymond, you are walking through the University quarter. The University of Toulouse was founded in 1229 by Count Raymond VII as part of his penance following the defeat of his House in the Albigensian Crusade, and is one of the great universities of France. It special-

St James, Eglise St Sernin, Toulouse

Streets of Toulouse

ises in law, medicine and science, as well as writing on walls, although some of the wall writings are quite amusing, and worth remembering. My heart goes out to one irate Anarchist who had scribbled up some sound revolutionary advice — "*Mangeons un flic*", "Let's eat a policeman"!

Through the student quarter then, to the Convent Les Jacobins. This has been recently restored and is a really beautiful building. Built in about 1230, it was the first home in France for the preaching friars of the Order of St. Dominic, endowed, like the University, from the fines imposed in settlement of the Albigensian Crusade. The name 'Jacobin' incidentally, is often applied to the Dominican houses because their first establishment, in Paris, was by the Port St. Jacques, through which, of course, the pilgrims passed out on the road to Compostella.

Like most of the Toulouse churches, this one was fortified and

Public Gardens, Toulouse

the inside is a vast, cool, golden building, with two naves, and the double vault is completed with circling stone pillars of the *palmier*, the palm roof, so called because the arches and buttresses do indeed resemble the trunk and leaves of a palm tree. This church has to be visited and contains, as a principal relic, the head of St. Thomas Aquinas.

A little way past the Jacobins lies the bank of the Garonne and the Place de la Daurade. This, apart from the Church of Notre Dame la Daurade, has many fine town houses, or *hôtels*, the homes of the merchants of *pastel*. Pastel is, to put it simply, woad. This indelible blue dye, much beloved, or so we are told, by the Ancient Britons, was also used to dye the purple robes of the Roman emperors and senators and, for the first 1500 years of the Christian era, the vestments of Holy Church. The Reformation, and the discovery in the 16th century of another dye, indigo, which comes from the East Indies, dealt two crippling blows to the pastel trade, and it collapsed. Only the fine Renaissance houses of the merchants remain as a reminder of what was once a hugely successful industry.

The Church of La Daurade contains a black virgin, Notre Dame La Noire, and is also the church for the benediction of the Jeaux Floraux — the floral games — the oldest artistic prize in Europe.

Languedoc, as we have noted, was the home of the troubadours, and although they faded away after the Albigensian Crusade, which was nothing to sing about, their influence lived on. In 1323, seven troubadours who intended to revive the arts of their prececessors, founded a company of artists which they called the *Gay-Savoir*. A contest, rather like an eisteddfod, was held each May and the winner received, as a prize, a golden violet. The company was endowed by a wealthy widow, Clemence Isaure, in 1490, and Louis XIV placed it on a firm foundation by establishing the Academy of the Jeux Floreaux, which still exists under the protection of the local administration, maintaining the artistic inheritance of the '*langue-d'oc*. They still administer the festival arts, a continuation of artistic effort still going strong after 650 years.

Near La Daurade incidentally, is an excellent restaurant, *La Cassoulet*, which is named after the town's great gastronomic offering, even if Castelnaudry claims to produce the definitive version of the dish.

Cassoulet is a rich, filling stew of sausage, beans and bacon, steamed in an earthenware pot over an open fire. Personally, I find it too filling, a meal in itself, and prefer that other local delicacy, *Canard Magré*, a duck cutlet, with a good Madeiran wine from Béarn, perhaps at the nice little restaurant, *La Bascoule*, on the *quai* near the Canal du Midi.

Turning back into the centre of the town, down the Rue de Metz, you will come to the cathedral of St. Etienne. This is a rather untidy structure, erected a bit at a time from the 11th to the 17th centuries, in a mixture of classical styles. It is imposing enough and as well as some fine tapestries contains the tomb of

Pierre-Paul Riquet, who built the Canal du Midi from Toulouse to Sète in the 17th century. Apart from that it has little of interest. You may, I fancy, have had enough of churches by now, so for a look at the sights and shops of modern Toulouse, head back down the Rue de Metz, past the Musée des Augustines, and turn down the Rue des Changes.

The Rue des Changes, now a pedestrian precinct, is one of the oldest streets in the town, and was once the finance and banking section. One old building still bears the emblem of those thrifty hard-working creatures, the bees, while if you poke into any side alley or courtyard, you will find untouched, and frequently crumbling, many once-proud *hôtels*, their old wooden galleries and staircases rotting away from neglect.

The Rue des Changes and its continuation, the Rue St. Rome, is full of little shops, boutiques, artisans' workshops and galleries, all thronged with a busy crowd of customers, and this leads at last, back to the wide trottoirs and cafés of the Place du Capitole.

Modern Toulouse earns its bread by commerce, by the university, and by industry, notably aviation. The Sud-Aviation, now Aerospatiale aircraft manufacturers, have their works here, busy with a new breed of aircraft, notably the Concorde, and aviation has deep roots in Toulouse. If you look across the Place du Capitole, you will see, on the corner of the Rue du Taur, the hotel where Antoine St.-Exupery and his colleagues stayed between their mail-flights to Morocco, about which St.-Exupery wrote so vividly.

As a student centre, Toulouse is naturally full of museums and has a lively artistic life with a theatre, many cinemas and art galleries, while the Jacobins and St. Etienne are used regularly for orchestral performances. The students make up over ten percent of the population and provide custom for a host of little bars, restaurants and cabarets. All in all, Toulouse is an agreeable town in spite of the rantings on the walls, and if they do no more than remind us of the undercurrents, they serve some purpose.

Toulouse has one great link with political struggle of a more deadly sort, for it was here that Voltaire, almost single-handed, finally forced the government of France to act over the Calas

In the Rue des Changes

affair, one of the gravest acts of injustice in the history of France.

*　　*　　*　　*

One of the great advantages of European travel is that it re-opens the door to the history of significant people and events, and by any standards, few Europeans, one might well say few human beings, have been more interesting than Voltaire.

In Britain he is best known as a playwright and the author of '*Candide*', and many Englishmen will assure each other that '*all's for the best in the best of all possible worlds*' or that it's necessary to do something drastic '*pour encourage les autrés*', without much idea of the author of those sentiments.

The English — not the British — owe Voltaire a deeper debt, for he was the first notable Frenchman to disabuse his country-men of the conviction that the English were a barbarous race, liv-ing in a fog-shrouded island. Voltaire liked the English, mainly for their deep and fundamental sense of justice, and there can be little doubt that the Calas affair opened his eyes to a native lack of this necessary virtue.

Jean Calas, a man of fifty-five, was a Huguenot who in 1767 lived in Toulouse with his family which included a son, Paul, a boy of fourteen. Paul was a manic-depressive, notably unstable, and when one day he was found drowned, suicide was the obvi-ous conclusion. Not obvious enough, apparently, for the magis-trates of Toulouse. Calas and his entire family, including his young daughters, were arrested and kept shackled in prison. Calas himself, after strenuously denying the charge of murder, was brutally tortured by order of the court, and after a travesty of a trial condemned to be broken at the wheel in the place outside St. Sernin. This elderly man was taken out, lashed across a cart-wheel and his arms and legs smashed with iron bars. Death from shock took several hours. His wife was imprisoned, and his daughters forcibly confined in a Catholic convent. All this took place, remember, not in the barbarous Middle Ages, but in the late years of the 18th century.

Calas's other son had, however, managed to escape and made

his way to Switzerland. From there he contacted Voltaire and told the story. It is significant that the boy felt that only Voltaire could assist his family, and Voltaire did. He contacted everyone he could, in any position of authority, he wrote letters, he organized petitions, he badgered, he pleaded, he demonstrated, and he won.

He could not restore the life, but he did reverse the verdict. The family were released and compensated, and the magistrates dismissed from office. When the new ones committed a similar denial of justice some years later, lawyers being intransigent by nature, Voltaire rose up again in defence of the innocent, and yet again, he won. Toulouse gave Voltaire his most lasting reputation.

In France then, Voltaire is not surprisingly regarded as something rather more than the creator of Pangloss and Candide. He is the eternal reminder than the individual matters. The French are nothing if not individualistic, and when Voltaire died, they inscribed on his tomb, "*He taught us to be free*". There have been worse epitaphs.

* * * *

Before we leave Toulouse, with its art, its terror and its politics, to point out the fact that life here, if studious and intense is not always so serious, one last wall slogan: "*Lisez Rimbaud et mourier*". Only a French student could write that.

7

The Rouergue

To the east of Quercy lies the Rouergue. Broadly speaking, it coincides with the modern département of Aveyron, which takes its name from the river Aveyron, the course of which we shall follow for much of this chapter. The Aveyron rises in the causse country, a little below Sévérac, and wanders west for eighty miles or so until it runs into the Tarn near Moissac. It is not an imposing river, yet it has its moments, and we can follow it upstream to the east and visit some pleasant places.

Leaving Moissac and passing again through Negrepelisse, we then run out of Quercy and into the Rouergue at a spot a little beyond Montricour, under the walls of the great castle of Bruniquel.

According to legend, or more precisely to Gregory of Tours, Bruniquel was built by that warlike Merovingian queen, Brunéhaut, who when quite an old lady was murdered by her own kinsfolk in the dynastic wars of the later Visigoths. It's all rather unlikely, since the existing château built of an agreeable yellow weathered stone only dates from about 1200, long after Brunéhaut was killed, and towering on a cliff above the Aveyron it was actually built to guard the eastern marches of Quercy. The central keep, the *Tour Brunéhaut*, is in good condition and can be visited, although the rest of the castle is crumbling, while the village itself is well worth seeing, a perfect medieval *bourg* with

94

Bruniquel

narrow cobbled streets and tottering houses, glowing in the morning sun.

Bruniquel has, it appears, more recent claims to fame, for as I got from my car an elderly gentleman rose from his seat and informed me that here they made '*le vieux fusil*'.

"Oh good!" I said, "A cannon factory, that makes a change." I had had rather enough of churches. Considerable confusion then followed. *Le Vieux Fusil*, it appears, is a film, a motion picture. I have in fact been trying to see it since that morning, without success, so it is not clearly a *success d'estime* in cinematographic terms. Be that as it may, it clearly brightened the lives of the good people at Bruniquel. It is, I gather, the story of a man, the owner of a castle occupied by the Nazis, who uses his knowledge of the place and its secret passages, to wage war on the occupiers. My guide was at great pains to show me who stood where and who said what, so should you ever get the chance to see *Le Vieux Fusil*, you can see, at the same time, beautiful Bruniquel and many of the inhabitants.

*   *   *   *

St Antonin-Noble-Val

La Maison de L'Amour, St Antonin

Little Penne, further up the valley, is a stranger to fame, yet very lovely. It is quite small, slowly dying in fact, with less than five hundred inhabitants now, a vision of golden walls, flat red roofs, and a great castle which hangs out over the river valley, defying gravity. The village was built in the shadow of the fortress in the 13th century and is full of lovely medieval houses, with wooden galleries and sculptured stone porches, a perfect prelude to the trip through the gorges of the Aveyron up to St. Antonin.

There are two roads up to St. Antonin, one along the river, which leads the traveller through tunnels in the rocks, the other over the *corniche*, which gives some fine views before descending to lead you over the bridge into the delightfully named St. Antonin-Noble-Val, under the bold buttresses of the Roc d'Anglers.

At St. Antonin, the Aveyron is joined by a tributary, the little Bonnet, which flows in and under the town, along rivulets by the

97

houses, and is crossed within the town by scores of stone foot-bridges. St. Antonin is the oldest town in this part of the country, dating back to Roman times, and takes its name from the St. Anthony who preached the gospel to the pagan Gauls herea-bouts. The town began to grow about the year 1000 AD, when it was a centre for tanning hides and a market town for the western Rouergue.

The *Hotel de Ville*, largely constructed in 1125, is the oldest civic building in France, and today, as a museum, contains a fine collection of prehistoric relics. The town received a charter from St. Louis about 1227, and this led to a considerable commercial development, and as you will see, the building of some fine houses.

St. Antonin has very narrow streets so it is best to leave your car on the far side of the Aveyron and walk. One house not to be missed, in a little street beside the Hotel de Ville, is the so-called *Maison de L'Amour*.

I was ambling happily around in a thin rain when the little sculptured heads of a couple kissing caught my eye, carved above a window.

"*C'est La Maison de L'Amour*" said one of the two old men, talking by the footbridge.

"What was that, in the Middle Ages?" I asked, a question which produced lots of laughter.

"*Un bordel, M'sieu!*"

Well, perhaps! A medieval brothel is hardly an everyday event, and whatever its original function, La Maison de L'Amour, and St. Antonin Noble Val, were two memorable stops in my tour along the Aveyron, and a place I urge you to visit. Your reputation cannot suffer!

*   *   *   *

Pressing on up the valley to Varen, which has a massive castle and church in close combination, you have a choice, and because it's a nice run and to save retracing our steps, you can bear south here, at Lexos, and head for Cordes, on a hill above the little river

The Corniche above the Aveyron

Cérou. Cordes, even from a distance, is a striking place. It hugs the crown of a humped green hill like a helmet, and looks exactly what it is, a medieval fortified town.

It was built at the end of the Albigensian Wars by Count Raymond VII of Toulouse. It was, like the *bastides* which it closely resembles, a new town, built as a speculation, around the site of an old castle and hunting lodge of the Counts. Once the town was finished, the Count invited his subjects to live there, offering them in return, a charter, land for ploughing, freedom from taxes and customs dues, and for each household, a cow, a goat and an ox. The population grew, and as the name implies, it became a centre for *cordeliers*, workers in leather. The town survived the Wars of Religion and two outbreaks of the plague which decimated the population, and only fell into a decline in the present century. By the start of the Second World War, Cordes was virtually abandoned.

Cordes

It has survived, just, thanks to the effects of a group of artists who elected to live there, and it is now slowly recovering, with a growing community of artists, and an ever increasing number of visitors, drawn by its beauty and historic connections. For Cordes is beautiful and virtually unspoiled. Cars can only penetrate the town with difficulty and are best left at the Place de La Trinite, outside the main gate

Two roads lead into the centre of Cordes, the Chemin de Ronde, which runs by the ramparts, and the Grand Rue, or Rue de La Tour, which is the central street. Although the streets are lined with fine buildings, three in particular are well worth a mention; the house of the *Grand Veneur,* the Chief Huntsman, which is covered with carvings of animals and scenes of the chase; the *Grand Fauconnier*, the falconer, once the mews, decorated with carvings of falcons; and that of the *Grand Écuyer*, the Great Squire. On the eastern side of the town, past these three buildings, are the Paternoster Steps, built in the 16th century as a thanks offering for the ending of the plague, with one step for every word in the prayer.

In the town centre stands the Terrasse de La Bride, which offers stupendous views over the countryside, and the halls, built in the 14th century and still in occasional use as a market. The town well stands here and you will note, on a nearby pillar, a fine iron cross. It appears that during the 16th century the Bishop of Albi sent three Inquisitors to Cordes to root out heresy. The inhabitants took this visit most unkindly and threw the Inquisitors down the well, which is, according to a plaque on the wall, over 300 feet deep.

As you may imagine, I paled at yet another account of this popular local activity. Frankly, I rather doubt if, even in the heat of rage, the townspeople would foul their main water supply by drowning people in it, but why spoil a good yarn? The iron cross was erected as a penance and to serve as a perpetual reminder.

Cordes, shimmering in the hot sun, is a necessary stop for the visitor to the Rouergue and from there we turn north again, for Languépie, Najac and Villefranche, back once again, in short, to the Aveyron.

*   *   *   *

The well in Cordes

Languépie, surrounded by woods, is an agreeable spot, built by Bernard de Valady, Baron of Languépie, in about 1150. The château has stayed in the same hands, surviving fire, war and revolution, ever since. Languépie has two bridges across the Aveyron, which is joined here by the Viaur, and the local baron once gained a considerable income by charging two tolls, one to get into the town and another to get out. The Count of Toulouse was very impressed by this stratagem, but demanded fifty percent of the proceeds. A fine example of someone being too clever by half!

North of Languépie, mighty Najac stands proudly on its high green hill, a splendid sight and an instant attraction. The town and castle of Najac were built to command and defend the lower Rouergue and the original château was erected by Count Bertrand de St. Gilles in 1000 AD.

Najac is an interesting example of military architecture, for while the twin hills on which it stands command the valley, one is useless as a fortress without the command of the other. Therefore, the château stands on one, and the *bourg*, or walled town, on the other, while the lower town straggles across the col, or arête, that connects the two. There is a double row of houses along the ridge and built close together on the top of a steep cliff, they presented another defence line, a thousand feet along the valley crest.

The last independent Count of Toulouse was forced to marry his daughter to Alphonse de Poitiers, brother of St. Louis, who took the title when the old count died. Alphonse was a castle builder, architect of many fine *bastides*, and he turned his attention to Najac with a view to making it impregnable.

He pulled down the original castle and erected the present one in 1253. The castle was used to hold captive Knights Templar when the order was suppressed in 1307, and withstood many sieges during the Hundred Years War. It certainly wasn't impregnable. The English held it from 1362 to 1369, when they were thrown out. The Black Prince's captain, John Chandos, retook it in the same year, but his seneschal was swiftly evicted in 1370.

After the Hundred Years War, Najac served as a prison and

later as the administrative centre for the Lower Rouergue up to the Revolution of 1789, but nowadays the castle has fallen into ruin.

The town itself though, continues to prosper. It has a considerable tourist income, a 13th-century church, a good example of the Early Gothic, built as a fine on the townsfolk for participating in the Albigensian Crusade, while the streets with their colonnaded houses, echo to the tinkle of water from the large fountain, carved from one huge stone in about 1344, which has kept the townsfolk from thirst from then up to the present century.

* * * *

Najac

Fountain, Najac

Above Najac, a much bigger place altogether, lies Villefranche-de-Rouergue, another *bastide*, one of a series built to contain the English, inside Quercy and out of the Rouergue. Like Najac, Villefranche was built by the Counts of Toulouse, and then rebuilt by the indefatigable Alphonse de Poitiers in 1265.

Bastides have certain essential features, a double wall, or *enciente*, a fortified hiding place, perhaps a castle but more often the church, a many-arched market square with *cornières*, and narrow streets built on a rectangular plan. In the case of Villefranche, with the exception of the narrow straight streets, colonnaded square and fortified church, all the other fortification has gone. Today, Villefranche is a crowded, bustling place, with little time for retrospection on the part of the inhabitants. On the other hand, visitors are lucky, for the town is full of interesting sights, most of them relevant to the subject of this book.

Villefranche has always been a prosperous town. It stands at a natural junction, where the Aveyron swings round the base of the

105

The Aveyron

causse de Limogne, and many traders therefore set up shop here. It was also a stopping place on the road from Le Puy to Compostella, and thus served many pilgrims, and as a final bonus, silver was once mined locally. Charles V gave the town a mint and it became the capital of Haut-Guyenne, and contained a powerful garrison.

The main square, the Place Notre-Dame, has *bastide cornières* and is dominated by the immense bulk of the Church of Notre-Dame, which is strong enough to be a fortress, although it dates from 1620 when the wars were just over, but it was still built for defence.

The square slopes quite sharply, and if you walk up past the great iron cross and through the back streets of the old *bastide* quarter, you will come to the outer boulevard and the Church of the Black Penitents, a preaching order formed at the end of the Wars of Religion, around 1600. After the Wars of Religion it was

Place Notre-Dame, Villefranche

easy to seduce the nobility back to allegiance with bribes or invitations to Court, but the poor clung stubbornly to the Reformed Church, and as an arm of the Counter Reformation, various preaching Orders, like the Penitents, were established. The most famous and enduring were, of course, the Jesuits, but the Black Penitents, although long dispersed, were a force at the time. Their church has a pretty bell-tower and stands on the edge of the circling boulevard which marked the course of the old walls.

The jewel of Villefranche though, is the ancient Chartreuse of St. Saveur. This elegant little monastery with its adjoining pilgrim chapel, the *Chapelle des Etrangers* stands on the road to Albi, a little outside the town, on the old track to Compostella.

It was endowed in 1451, by one of the town's rich citizens and is the purest example of the Gothic. The Chartreuse is now a hospital, but it can be visited and the chapel and cloisters are in excellent condition. The chapel is linked with the Little Cloister, and

107

then through the refectory to the Grand Cloister. You will notice the stone lectern in the refectory, a reminder that during meal-times bible stories were read to the assembled brethren. Thirteen houses once surrounded the Grand Cloister, which is said to be one of the largest of its kind in France.

*   *   *   *

North of Villefranche past the beautiful chateau of St. Rèmy, lies the next link in Alphonse de Poitiers' chain of military towns, the *bastide* town of Villeneuve. You will notice that many of the *bastides* are called Villeneuve or Villefranche and that even if they are old towns to us today, they were once new towns and fine examples of town planning. Unlike modern new towns, the *bastides* are beautiful.

This one, Villeneuve-d'Aveyron, is an older town than the name implies, for the church there was commenced about 1100 to celebrate the capture of Jerusalem at the end of the First Crusade, and is one of only two French churches dedicated to the Holy

Sauveterre de Rouergue, the 'cornieres'

The Château du Bosc, home of Toulouse Lautrec

Sepulchre. To help pay for the works, the Bishop of Rodez allowed the town a market, which still exists today. By 1249 Villeneuve had 3500 inhabitants, a considerable population for those days, and was already fortified.

Villeneuve today is an old narrow town with cobbled streets, a typical bastide, with all the usual features, but with huge fortifications and powerful gates. A good hotel to stay in while visiting these parts is the Auberge de La Tour, a *Logis de France*, opposite the main gateway, the Tour Savignac.

From Villeneuve, we turn south and east to run across the country to yet another *bastide*, Sauveterre de Rouergue. Sauveterre is another popular *bastide* name, but unlike the others I visited, Sauveterre was almost deserted and has few inhabitants. This *bastide* has retained its defences and as it was the base of the Seneschal of Rouergue, William of Mâcon, who kept his garrison troops there, they were particularly fine to begin with. The central square is very large and made almost eerie by a complete absence of people. Only one old man limped slowly across it — a sad reminder of increasing depopulation.

Arriving in Sauveterre puts us on the doorstep of the Albigeois, and it is only a short drive on our way there to visit the Château du Bosc, seat of the Lautrec family and once the childhood home of the artist, Henri de Toulouse-Lautrec. This beautiful and peaceful chateau, with its warm red shutters and strutting fantail pigeons, is a far cry indeed from the streets of Paris and the music of the Moulin-Rouge.

Lautrec was born in Albi, but the family lived at Bosc, as they still do, and much of the artist's childhood was spent here. The present château was constructed around the ancient *château-fort*, and you can visit it during the summer months, parking in the courtyard by the poulter-pigeons and going inside to inspect the artist's bedroom, and see the Salle de Garde of the old fort, and some of the fine tapestries and furniture which the house contains. The family are often in residence and you may, if you are lucky, have a descendant of Lautrec to show you around.

We shall see and hear more of Lautrec at our next stop, Albi, so this visit will serve as a foretaste of the future. We turn south now, then leaving the Aveyron to retrace its steps up to the Causse de Sévérac, and heading past the viaduct at Viaur and Carmaux, we arrive at the Tarn, and the great red brick city of the Albigeois.

8

Albi and the Albigeois

The countryside of the Albigeois, which lies, naturally enough around the city of Albi, covers a considerable area and runs roughly north-east to south-west from its northern boundary, the rivers Aveyron and Viaur, to the Montagne Noire. Albi lies in the middle, and is the best central spot for touring, at least to begin with, until you move out along the Tarn.

The Albigeois is river country, with three major streams flowing across it from the Cévennes, or the Great Causses. These are, from the south, the Agout which is fed by two tributaries, the Arn and the Gijou; across the centre flows the Dadou which joins the Agout above Lavaur; and finally the colourful Tarn on which stands the great red city of Albi itself.

This is the middle Tarn, free from the picturesque gorges of Lozére and therefore flowing more slowly, but still a beautiful river dividing the rolling hills of the country around Cordes from the more open regions to the south of the city. The Albigeois is not mountainous and in the main only lightly forested, but there is no real lack of rolling wooded hills, with considerable forests to the north-west above Gaillac and more in the south along the slopes of Montagne Noire and in the Languedoc National Park.

Albi, the capital of the region is, like Toulouse, a brick-built city. All along the Tarn, anywhere west of the Cévennes, brick replaces stone as the main building material, but here it is not the

Albi

prosaic brick of the north. This is a deep, burning, red, glowing brick, that seems to heat the air around it, glowing like a dull fire when the sun shines on it.

Albi is now an agricultural centre, marketing wine and wheat, but it was established a thousand years ago, primarily as a religious centre and as the seat of a powerful bishopric. Albi gave its name to the Albigensian heretics and therefore to the Albigensian Crusade which devastated Languedoc in the early 13th century. In the second half of that century, after the last Cathars had been put to death at Montsegur in Ariège, the Bishops of Albi began to build the palace and cathedral which are the present pride of the city. Both were largely paid for from the fines of former heretics, and both were built for war. Bishop Bernard de Combret built the fortress-palace of La Berbie beside the Tarn, between 1254 and 1270, and his successor, Bernard de Castanet, began to build the great Cathedral of St. Cecilia about 1280. First things first, you see.

Present day Albi is just the right size for a city, with about

Cathedral and 'baldaquin', Albi

50,000 inhabitants and approached from the North, across the Pont 22nd Aout, the visitor gets a first impressive view of red roofs and yellow walls, all dominated by the massive walls of palace and cathedral. You only get one chance to make a first impression and Albi makes the most of it. You can park near the cathedral and most of the town's major attractions are close at hand, and a tourist route round them has been marked out by the *Syndicate d'Initiative.*

The cathedral is a vast mountain of soaring red brick. The south door is sheltered by a massive decorated stone porch or *baldaquin*, and reached by a flight of steps. Inside, the cathedral is richly decorated and unlike most French cathedrals seems to have been spared destruction in the Wars of Religion or the Revolution. It took over a hundred years to complete and stands on the former site of a Romanesque abbey. It was, even so, ahead of its time, for Albi did not become an archbishopric until 1678, and this great building must have seemed very imposing for a single See.

St. Cecilia's is one of those churches which has to be visited, for while many are very similar and in succession even boring, St. Cecilia's is full of paintings, carvings and a magnificent rood screen. The frescoes, notably from the Renaissance when Louis d'Amboise took charge of the building and built the splendid bell tower, were executed by Italian craftsmen, hired to decorate the interior in the style of the Quattrocento.

Originally, the cathedral was designed to double up as a fortress and in this role it adjoins the Bishop's palace, La Berbie, which was at first a pure castle with a high *enceinte* and half-a-dozen protective towers. The cathedral next door is built so close to the riverside cliff that there is no west door, and the blank wall is, of course, defensive.

Much of this military work was pulled down in the 18th century and since 1922 the palace has served as a gallery, dedicated mainly to the works of Toulouse-Lautrec. The exhibition is the most complete collection of the artist's work, the gift of Lautrec's mother, the Comtesse de Toulouse-Lautrec, and his close friend Maurice Joyant. Albi is very proud to have been the birthplace of

114

such a painter and the municipality has added to the collection at every opportunity.

It contains over 600 examples of his work, including 200 paintings and many lithographs, a fine cross-section of the artist's work and has, in addition, works by Dufy, Bonnard, Matisse, Utrillo, Roualt, and many, many more. The gallery of Toulouse-Lautrec in Albi is, not to put too fine a point on it, stunning, a credit to the town and its inhabitants.

Henri de Toulouse-Lautrec was born in the Hôtel du Bosc, the family's town house in Albi, in 1864. He was the eldest son of Count Alphonse de Toulouse-Lautrec Monfa, a descendant of the great Counts of Toulouse, and Adele de Celeyran who, apart from being the Count's wife was also his cousin. When Henri was fourteen he had a fall in the Hôtel du Bosc and broke both his legs. The bones were slow to knit, and when in 1879 he had another accident, the damage was such that his legs refused to mend and became permanently shortened. It is supposed that the consanguinity of his parents was the reason for this.

Henri had always been artistic and his injuries and the resulting prolonged convalescences gave him ample time to develop his skills. In 1882 Lautrec went to Paris, settled in the artist's quarter of Monmartre, where he began, as is well known, a career of great brilliance and a life of considerable debauchery.

What is less well know is that he remained attached to his family and to his native Albigeois. He returned home most years for a holiday, and when the life he was leading reduced him to serious illness, his mother, who loved him dearly, would go to Paris and bring him home, begging him to find subjects close at hand, in the countryside or in the old southern towns like his friend Cezanne. But it was no good. "I am a painter of the streets, and of the city," he said. So he was, and so he remained until his death in 1901. He was only thirty-seven.

The Hôtel de Bosc, his birthplace, is in a little street near the cathedral. It contains many relics from the artist's childhood, and can be visited, during a walk around the artist's centre of the town. The houses of old Albi have been transformed in recent years and many are now workshops, ateliers, or galleries, for a wide range of creative effort, while others have become boutiques or restaurants.

Off the Rue Ste.-Maries, down from the cathedral, are the church and cloisters of St. Salvy, a quiet little spot off a busy street which leads through to the Lices, formerly a tilt-yard, and the gardens which lead of the Lices Jean Moulin, making a pleasant pathway back to the cathedral. On the way you will pass the statue of another native of the town, the navigator Lapérouse, who lost his life exploring the East Indies in 1788.

*   *   *   *

Albi makes a good centre for excursions along the Tarn, particularly to the east towards Ambialet and Valence d'Albigois.

Ambialet is a most picturesque spot, a village and castle perched on an island between two arms of the river, and from there you can swing north to Valence, before returning to Albi through Carmaux. It makes a nice run, and you should lunch at Ambialet.

*   *   *   *

The land along the Tarn west of Albi is wine country and the road to it runs first of all through Castelnau de Lévis, which gives fine views back over Albi, and across the great lake at Marssac, before arriving at Gaillac.

The vineyards of Gaillac spread over a very wide area and embrace the wines of Gaillac proper, the best of which are white, *pétillant*, and delicious, and the more robust vintages of the Cotes du Tarn. The total area is about 50,000 acres and it produces a vast quantity of wine. I enjoy the Gaillac whites very much, especially the '*Perle*', which goes very well with poultry, trout and crayfish from the local rivers. A good restaurant at which to try wine and food is the *Maison du Vigneron* on the Toulouse road.

Gaillac itself is very much a wine centre, with coopers busily making barrels in the backstreet workshops. Like all Tarn towns, it is built mainly of brick, with many little squares each with its

Gaillac

fountain and overhanging houses. It has the usual abbatical church, this one dating from the 7th century, and an interesting Natural History Museum.

A short distance away lies Lisle-sur-Tarn, once a *bastide* and still retaining a market place with typical *cornières*, and Lisle is a good centre for touring the western Albigois, especially if you stay at the *Princinor Hotel*, which recalls how our own Black Prince once toured these parts — with an army of 20,000 men.

The castle of St. Géry, below Lisle, is a fine place, dating from the 14th century but continually built up and altered until the end of the 18th century when the then seigneur lost his head to the guillotine. His wife found some flaw in the indictment, and although the Count lost his head, the family kept the castle

Rabastens, on the border of the Albigeois is a busy little place with a nice little church, the Notre-Dame-de-Bourg, and a very good hotel, the *Pre-Vert*. Just below Rabastens the tributary riv-

117

ers Dadau and Agout join before flowing into the Tarn, and here we turn back through Lavaur and Graulhet to Lautrec.

Graulhet, like many towns hereabouts, is a tanning centre, but unlike the others, it is a place to hurry through as quickly as possible. Any town that can process 35 million animal skins in one year is best avoided!

Lautrec, once owned by the Knights Hospitaller and then by the ancestors of Toulouse-Lautrec, is much prettier, but need not detain us long and we can press on to Castres.

* * * *

It would be unfortunate if any traveller approaching Castres followed the customary route 'Toutes Directions' and circled the town without stopping. Pleasant and shady though the plane-tree lined boulevards are, Castres is well worth a stop. It stands on the Agout which, flowing under a series of bridges, has galleried houses leaning over its course all the way through the centre of the town. It is a centre for the wool industry and is an excellent centre for the southern Albigeois and the Montagne Noire.

Castres is an old town. The Romans had a marching camp here and the Benedictines founded a monastery on the site of the present cathedral of St. Benoit in about 850 AD and for much of its history the town, under the lordship of Albi, was ruled by consuls, like Toulouse. More recently it is renowned as the birthplace of Jean Jaurès.

The French are much given to naming streets after their political heroes and there can be few, if any towns in France, that do not somewhere recall Gambetta, or Jean Moulin, who organised the Resistance, or Jean Juarès.

As his birthplace, Castres goes one better than the norm, with a *Place Jean Juares* and a fine statue, and a museum.

Juarès was in some respects a successor of Gambetta and born in Castres in 1859. He was twelve at the outbreak of the Franco-Prussian war in 1870, and the later suppression of the Paris Commune, so he grew up during the early years of the Third Republic

118

Jean Juarés, Castres

and became one of the founding fathers of the French Socialist Party.

Juarès was no stereotyped political demagogue however. France has never been short of those. He came out boldly in defense of Dreyfus, which was an unpopular thing to do, and Juarès was, besides being a politician, a professor of philosophy first at Albi and later at Toulouse. He was also an ardent pacifist and protested strongly against the growing demands for *revanché* that led up to the Great War, with the result that he was assasinated in Paris by a fanatic on the eve of the outbreak of war, on the 31st July 1914.

Overlooking the Agout, Castres

You can park in the Place Jean Juarès and if you do so, and stay at a nearby hotel, you will have most of the town's attractions within easy walking distance. Go first to the quai by the Agout and see the old houses overlooking the river, before walking past the market hall, and the fine equestrian statue of Jeanne d'Arc, then past the church of St. Benoit to the Hôtel de Ville.

This was once the Bishop's Palace, although much reconstructed in 1700. You go under an arched gateway, with a beautiful sundial on the pediment, to enter the Palace itself, and if you walk straight through, you will arrive in the episcopal gardens.

These were laid out by the Le Notre in about 1660, and with the trimmed *boiserie* and sparkling fountain, are very beautiful.

The Hôtel-de-Ville contains the Musée Jean Juarès, where several rooms contain memorabilia, papers, letters, possessions of various kinds, all relating to the politician, and the fine Musee Goya, an excellent collection of Spanish paintings from the 15th to the 17th centuries, left to the town in 1894 by a local artist and collector Marcel Brigabol.

Apart from his masterpiece, *The Phillipine Junta*, which he painted in 1814, the museum contains over 100 other Goyas, including many scenes from the Peninsular during the Napoleonic wars, in the period 1809 to 1814. Brigabol was a lifelong admirer of Goya and this collection must be one of the most representative collections of the artist's work anywhere in the world.

Many of the central streets in Castres have been transformed into pedestrian precincts and it is a most pleasant little town to stroll around in.

A short distance north-east of Castres, lies the rock "chaos" of Sidobre, a wilderness of lakes, waterfalls, rivers, granite gorges and curious wind-carved stones. It covers a considerable area and to get to the great attraction, the Roc d'Oie, a huge rock that looks for all the world like a big goose, and back again, is a day's excursion. Le Sidobre is another of those little-known areas, well worth a visit, full of natural attractions, completely unspoiled and largely unvisited. Beyond Sidobre our road leads on to Brassac and Lacaune.

Sundial, Hotel de Ville, Castres

Brassac lies on the Agout, and just within the confines of the *Parc Natural Region du Haut Languedoc*. This little town, with only 1500 inhabitants, has had a colourful tradition, dating back to the Gauls. It was completely destroyed by the Arabs in the 8th century and the ruins of their Moorish fort, the Castel-Sarrazy, still overlook the town. A little north of Brassac lies Castelnau, long time rival of Brassac, and during the Middle Ages a place famous for the manufacture of armour. The people of Castelnau took and sacked Brassac during the Wars of Religion, when there was no love lost between the towns. The Great Condé took Castelnau in turn and put it to the torch, while Brassac later became the headquarters of the brigand chief Baccou, who is said to have been so successful that when he sacked a city "he left nothing but the walls".

Both places are dreamy little towns today, devoted to spinning and weaving and all that ardent history seems a very long time ago.

The road from Brassac to Lacaune leads through mountainous country and past the great reservoir, the Lac de la Ravière. Lacaune is a centre for sheep rearing. The wool goes to the weavers of Brassac, the skin to the glove makers of Millau and the milk to the cheese of Roquefort. As with Sidobre, the countryside around Lacaune is little known and well worth exploring.

*   *   *   *

The southern boundary of the Albigeois is La Montagne Noire, the Black Mountains. It is in fact a range of mountains, the last rocky outcrop of the Cévennes, a long spur running southwest into the Minervois, averaging about 1000 metres in height and this barrier is the cause of some curious climatic effects.

The northern slopes are cold and thickly wooded with those dark conifers that give the range its name, while the southern slopes are warm, the escarpment providing a barrier against the chill eastern winds from the Massif Central and acting as a watershed for the Minervois. Riquet, who built the Canal du Midi, tapped the numerous streams of the Montagne Noire, to water his canal and fed many of them into the reservoir at St. Ferreol. The region is full of worthwhile visits, but is primarily a wilderness, part of the Languedoc National Park, and a paradise for the walker and camper.

From Castres a road leads down to St. Pons, which lies between the north face of the Montagne Noire and the southern slopes of Sidobre and the mountains of the Espinouse.

The first stop, Mazamet, is another wool town, from which a steep and interesting road leads up over the Montagne Noire to Carcassonne. I have been up on the top here, late on a clear night and seen the illuminated walls of Carcassonne glowing in the dark valley like a far-off jewel.

Past Mazamet lies the village of St. Amans-Soult, birth and burial place of one of Napoleon's greatest Marshals, the one who outlived them all and died in 1851, thirty years after his Emperor had died on St. Helena. The Marshal's tomb is on the right-hand

124

The Cathedral, St. Pons

side of the church. Soult visited England several times after the wars were over and became a personal friend of the Duke of Wellington.

We are running out of the Albigeois now and we leave it behind officially at a spot a little past La Bastide-Rouairoux, passing on to stop, and end this chapter at St. Pons.

This old city, with its massive fortified cathedral, echoed to the shrill cries of the town's majorettes, who were whistling, marching, and twirling their batons, hard at practice in the place behind the cathedral. No French town today is complete without its troupe of majorettes, little girls of all shapes and sizes who march in every procession, secular or religious, before the admiring eyes of their relatives. The best I have ever seen, and those hardly little girls, was made up of a French Rugby Fifteen, all tricked out with the essential batons, white boots and miniskirts, and led by a whistling giant with a great black beard. They were hilarious — and very well drilled! With that cheerful memory I left the children to it, and went to bed.

125

9

The Espinouse and the Great Causses

At St. Pons, the road divides. One route runs off south to Béziers and the Languedoc Littoral, but we continue to the east, along the valley, beneath the jutting mountains of the Espinouse. These mountains are surprising. Somehow one expects grandeur in the Alps or the Pyrénées, or somewhere well known but the Espinouse is virtually unknown, quite desolate, and spectacular.

The mountains are magnificent soaring peaks, with steep cliffs and deep narrow valleys, each sheltering a red-roofed village. They are not high, only running up to about 1000 metres, but they are very rugged and, as with the Montagne Noire, possessed of two different climates; cold and windswept to the north, mild and sheltered to the south. The Espinouse is a sun trap and all manner of exotic fruits and plants take root there and flourish. You may gather that I like the place.

The road runs along the valley of the Juar beside the river to the pretty village of Olargues, with its packhorse bridge and medieval tower. We are now inside Hérault, a *département* of Languedoc-Roussillon, and Olargues is a good spot to stay in while touring the Espinouse, a job that requires good brakes on the car and better nerves in the driver.

The Espinouse is another outcrop of the Massif Central and lies between the Agout, which waters the Albigeois, and the Juar, a tributary of the Orb. Much of it lies inside the area of the

The Espinouse

Languedoc National Park, an area of great natural beauty, preserved for the nation since 1972. The area is best explored on foot, or horseback, but there are many minor roads crossing the range and they take you through some beautiful scenery.

A little past Olargues the river Orb comes in from the east to be joined by the Juar and the Heric, and turn south for the sea at Valras-Plage.

The gorge of the Heric is worth exploring, as it leads up into the Espinouse and I would advise anyone to tour up the lovely valley of the Orb, but for the moment we go south to Roquebrun.

This is a piece of pure indulgence, since it lies outside the boundaries of this book, but it is so beautiful, and near at hand, that it would take a stronger will than mine to pass it by. The Orb is wide here, dammed by a small weir and with the sparkling river as a threshhold and the mountains as a backdrop, Roquebrun is a picture.

127

Olargues, on the Jaur

The roofs are overlooked by the medieval donjon, and apart from its beauty, Roquebrun is a perfect example of how the mountains hereabouts affect the climate. It is spring all the year round in Roquebrun.

The mimosa flowers here in February, when there is ice and snow in the col, only a thousand feet above. Oranges, lemons, even pineapples and bananas grow here, warmed by the sun and sheltered by the escarpment.

I have camped by the river at Roquebrun in November weather, and found it warm, but all this is, as I say, an indulgence, and we must retrace our steps back up the Orb to Tarrassac and turn east for Lamalou-les-Bains.

The Orb rises in the Causse de Larzac and is one of those lovely unexplored little rivers with many pretty villages studded along its path. Lamalou is a spa and has been so since Roman times. In the last century the little town was much frequented by artists and writers, and there is a present link with the literary scene, for if you travel north you will see, over to the west, the *Fôret des Écri-vains Combattants*, the Forest of Fighting Writers. This was planted to the memory of over five hundred French writers who fell in the Second World War, and their memorial is marked by a stone cross.

The road presses on to Bedarieux which, in spite of being larger is not as interesting as little Boussagues, a little to the north. This was the site of a Roman fortress, built by Caesar as a bulwark against the warlike tribe of the Ruthenois, who lived around what is now Rodez. There was a military road along the valley which took supplies to Spain from the *Provincia Romana*, which is now Provence, and this same road was used later by Compostella pilgrims coming in from Italy and St. Gilles. The village still has some medieval fortifications and is very picturesque.

North of Boussagues, a road veers off north-west and if we follow it along the course of the Orb, and past the dam at Avene, climbing steadily, we will arrive at the great pass, the Col Nôtre-Dame, that marks the boundary between Hérault and Aveyron, and so brings us once again, back within our chosen boundaries. There is a statue of the Virgin at the pass, and some stupendous views back to the jagged Espinouse far to the south, and across to the high escarpments to the causse country of the east. Our course runs north, past Montagnol and the fortress of St. Jean and St. Paul, to the caves of Roquefort.

*　*　*　*

General de Gaulle once wearily remarked that it was difficult to govern a country that produced three hundred different sorts of cheese, but I feel sure that if political necessity had compelled him to reduce this number to one, that one would be Roquefort.

The cheese of Roquefort has been a delicacy since pre-Roman times and parts of the caves of Roquefort, where the cheeses mature, were constructed by the orders of the Caesars. Roquefort *ville* clings to the sides of a massive fault in the Causse de Larzac.

It is quite small, with only 1300 inhabitants, but they staff the dairies of some fourteen cheese manufacturers, and between

129

them produce sixteen thousand tons of cheese each year. It cannot be a labour intensive industry.

The milk for all this comes from a million sheep grazing on the neighbouring Causse and, once this milk has been processed into cheeses, they are placed on racks in the caves under the Causse to mature. There is some element in the air, or some exhalation from the rocks that produces a growth, a blue-ing of the cheese to give it that special sharp tang. Roquefort cheese is delicious, and its special quality can seemingly be produced nowhere else.

Many others have tried to imitate it and two quite acceptable cheeses produced locally are the Bleu de Causse, and the Bleu d'Auvergne. They are good and much cheaper. Cheese lovers will also, in the course of this journey, be able to try St. Nectaire from the Auvergne, and Cantal from Aurillac. Chèvre, or goat's cheese, or *cabecous*, as they call it in the *patois*, can be found all over this part of the Midi, and since we have arrived at a suitable spot, it might be as well to discuss food and wine.

* * * *

I heard a travel broadcast on the radio recently and the speaker remarked that his family, when planning their camping holidays in France, spent all winter collecting tins of food for use on holiday and thereby avoided eating out in France at all. This was presented as a Good Idea! Well, *chaque a son metier*, but if the French have contributed anything to civilization, it is surely great cuisine, and the very idea of not eating local French food strikes me as shocking. Besides, it isn't so expensive if you balance price and value, and the reason that I, for one, camp in France, is that it enables me to spend some money on a good evening meal.

Granted that a family of four would not be able to eat out every day in France (or in England), there are certain ways of cutting the cost and enjoying the cooking.

I doubt if many visitors would want to eat two full scale meals a day. Personally, I cook myself a breakfast, have bread, cheese and wine for a picnic lunch, and go out to eat in the evening. Most French restaurants offer, apart from *à la carte*, a selection of menus, each containing four or five courses from 15 francs up, tax and service included. The most expensive menu is often *gastronomique*, offering a selection of regional specialities and often local wine. If you stick to the menus and the *vin du table*, the value will exceed the price.

Rabelais said that he knew of sixty ways to cook an egg, but then he was an extremist. On this journey we can sample a wide range of foods, dishes and cuisine, without going that far. The cuisine of Périgord is renowned in France and rates with that of Burgundy and Normandy, as the very best of French cooking. Elsewhere it varies, but there are always local dishes, fresh and filling, and others which if eaten elsewhere, would be an expensive luxury.

Practically anything from Périgord is correctly served with truffles and cooked in walnut oil. Goose and pâte are the local specialities. Toulouse has it *cassoulet*, and sausages, while Albi has tripe flavoured with saffron, trout, crayfish, and quail, all delicious. Ham and pâte from Lacaune and the Montagne Noire, and salmon from the Adour. Lamb and mutton come from the flocks on the causse; a *gigot* from Millau is a feast. For fresh fruit the region

The Causse Sauveterre, above Millau

Sheep on the Causse Larzac

is unequalled. Prunes from the Agenais; table grapes from Lafrancaise and Moissac, apples, pears, peaches from Quercy and the Tarn, strawberries from the Lot, all are reasonably priced and of superb quality.

Wines are available in abundance and if they lack the reputation of Bordeauz or Burgundy, it is promotion rather than quality that is the cause. Red wine from Cahors, whites from Gaillac, are well known. The wines of St. Chinian, below the Montagne Noire are excellent. The white wine from Estaing on the Lot is superb, while the rosé from Dunes on the Tarn is very good. The *gris-de-gris* Listel rosé of Hérault is my favourite wine and seemingly only available south of Toulouse. For a choice of wine, food and fruit, there is a lot to enjoy beyond the Dordogne.

*   *   *   *

A causse is a plateau. We saw that at Limogne, but the little

132

causses of Quercy are a world away from the great causses around Millau.

Millau, another town that lives off the sheep's back, lies on the Tarn at the foot of a great circle of causses. From the north-west these are: the Causse Sauveterre; the Causse Méjean; the Causse Noir; and the Causse Larzac. This last one we cross on the way north to Millau and it is by far the largest causse.

These causses are the result of volcanic eruption in the Massif Central, and the subsequent millenium of erosion. They are mainly of the Jurassic period and were once one immense slab, tilted south and west from the volcanoes of the Puy de Dôme. Then the rivers got to work, cutting down into the basalt, carving their way into deep gorges, while wind and weather seared away at the uplands above. The result is, in effect, a series of little deserts. If you dismiss the concept that a desert is necessarily composed of sand, the causse are deserts. They are desolate. They lack water and support only pastoral agriculture, notably sheep flocks and goats. Habitation is minimal for there is little water, and towns on the causse are non-existent. It might sound rather depressing, but the causses are beautiful. I am, admittedly, one of those desert-loving Englishmen, who find miles and miles of

The Causse Larzac

damn-all attractive, but even allowing for personal preferences, the causses are still beautiful. The earth cover is slight, but it supports a host of wild flowers. Given a little rain, or in the spring, they are a carpet of flowers, while in late summer, the slopes glow with deep purple heather and the air is like wine.

I have walked across the causse Larzac, following the pilgrim road on the Grande Randonée and found it a bracing experience. The stony ground made itself felt even through boots, while the close-knit thorns stripped the surface from the leather. However much townsfolk may have stared, my sombrero alone kept off the unrelieved glare of the sun, but did nothing for the heat bouncing off the rocks. At night the temperature fell rapidly and it was very lonely. The ground was too hard to get a tent peg in, but luckily the wind has eroded many shallow caves, giving excellent shelter and when it rains, which it did every day, you can fill your water bottle by holding it against channels or grooves in the rock. Apart from the occasional *lavogne*, or dewpond, there is little water on the high causse.

The causse, for all that, is not really lonely. It might be if you crave company, but if a little chat goes a long way there are frequent encounters with shepherds or shepherdesses — no anachronism here in the late 1970s, when the million sheep they guard up on the causse are the life support of the townspeople of the

The Caves at Roquefort

Millau

river valleys. Thanks to them, the causse country is in fact quite noisy, for all the sheep are belled, and move about in a deafening jangle. With this and the fact that the locals speak mainly the *langue d'oc patois*, social contact with any facility is limited to bobbing and smiling and trading shots of whisky for slices of strong goat's cheese. Northern French, the *langue d'oiel*, did not replace the *langue d'oc* in official correspondence until 1593, so it is not surprising that it still lingers in the villages.

A walk across any of the Great Causses is an enjoyable experience, given adequate preparation, and my brief experience is one I intend to repeat.

*   *   *   *

I rush ahead of myself. We were at Roquefort. The caves can be visited, and I arrived there on a Saturday morning just in time for the last tour of the week. It is fairly damp and chilly underground, and having visited many caves and grottoes in France, I went in wearing a fibre-pile jacket as well as an expectant expression.

It proved, as is too often the case, to be a traumatic experience. The only other visitors were a Swiss couple, she speechless, he inquisitive. His interest in the tour was such that I can only assume that, having visited the factory of Roquefort cheese, he intended to rush home and make one. How many sheep for how much milk? No! How much milk for how much cheese? Really! How long? How many? How much? Who? What? Where? When? How? And, having got an answer, he questioned it! A visit that normally takes twenty minutes took an hour and a half. Now, I have a very low boredom threshhold for statistics. After fifteen minutes of this I was drooping wearily against the walls. Trapped in the bowels of the earth with a manic Swiss and 400,000 maturing cheeses, is not the perfect way to spend a Saturday afternoon, *bien sûr*. Let us flee to Millau and the causses.

* * * *

From Millau, the causses tower over the town on every side, and indeed the best view of the town and the Tarn valley is obtained from the spot where the new road from the south carries round the causse de Larzac, and gives an eagle's-eye view over the valley.

The causse de Larzac, which we have just traversed is the largest of the great causses, and at some thousand metres above sea level is a pretty bleak prospect, even in summer.

It does, however, have some natural attractions and one I recommend is the Templar *cité* of La Couvertoirade, an untouched example of a Medieval *bourg*, from which the Knights Templar once guarded pilgrims across the causse. The River Dourbie and the minute causse Bégon divide causse Larzac from the causse Noir. This contains the curious rock chaos of Montpellier-le-Vieux, which is, be warned, simply a wilderness of rocks and difficult to get to. The causse Noir is forested and it is the dark pines that gave it a name.

The northern boundary of the causse Noir is the river Jonte which runs through a wide area open gorge, between Le Rozier and Meyreuis.

136

An excellent view of the Jonte can be obtained from Pyreleau opposite Le Rozier and if you cross the river here and head north up the gorge of the Tarn, you will have the causse Méjean on your right hand and the causse de Sauveterre rising up on your left.

The gorges of the Tarn lie outside the scope of this book, but they are well known and were described in my book on Languedoc Roussillon, for they lie mainly in Lozère.

There are a number of little tracks leading across the causses, and I advise you to pick the smallest you can and walk. The sense of space and sky up there is remarkable. It is sometimes hard to realise that this is in a populous state in Western Europe, and not some outpost of Mongolia.

On the causse Méjean, the great Maquis group of Bir Hakim had its base, until they were assaulted by a German S.S. regiment in 1944. The battle on the causse lasted two days, until the French position fell. The prisoners and wounded were taken into Mende and shot, some before their relatives in the town square, others in the little ravine outside the town. It's a harsh land in more ways than one.

* * * *

The last major causse, Sauveterre, lies north of the Tarn and several roads cross it, one to Mende in Lozère, the others up to La Canourgue. This town, just to make a change from the eternal

The Aveyron, near Sévérac

sheep, is an arable farming centre, and an important market for the sale of grain. It is a very old town, full of lovely buildings and an old church that was once the seat of a bishop.

Sauveterre itself, the village that names the causse, is a remarkable place with stout-walled stone houses clinging to the causse, the roofs tiled and almost flat, the eternal stone of the causse country protecting the few inhabitants from being scourged away by the ceaseless wind. It once contained a garrison of soldier-monks who added escort duties and the hanging of bandits to their normal priestly duties.

The last causse, of Sévérac, is gentler, green again like the little causse de Limogne, yet quite hilly, with white escarpments fringing the roads.

The Aveyron, that has accompanied us on much of our journey, rises here, a pretty stream as yet, running through flower-filled meadows, dominated all along the north road by the soaring hill and ruined castle at Sévérac-le-Château.

This was the seat, in the 17th century, of the unfortunate Lord Louis d'Arpajon, Marquis de Sévérac.

He served against the Moslems and soldiered valiantly in the armies of Louis XIII. His title was elevated into a dukedom and his wealth increased. He was a patron of the arts and sheltered in Paris his fellow swordsman, Cyrano de Bergerac. Louis, however, married unwisely, to a lively, lovely creature, for whom his mother developed a hatred. When his wife had a child, his mother persuaded him that the infant was not his. Louis murdered his wife and her supposed lover, and fled from France, his life and career in ruins. The great castle at Sévérac has since followed the same course and is now little more than a tumbledown heap of stones, where the clouds gather off the causse country and thunder rumbles away in the night.

10

The Olt, The Aubrac and Conques

West of La Canourgue and below the north face of causse de
Sévérac, lies the valley of the River Olt. It is, in fact, the Lot,
which is called the 'Olt' in the *patois* hereabouts. A whole string
of little riverside villages have 'olt' as a suffix, and if you were to
base yourself in any one of them, perhaps at one of the larger ones
like St. Geniez or St. Eulalie, then you have a good centre for touring on the causse Sévérac or the Fôret des Palanges to the south,
or into the Aubrac country which lies to the north.

The main route runs out to Rodez, but all minor roads lead
south to Le Pont and then on to the great lakes at Pont de-Salars
and Pareloup. These are artificial, and the result of hydro-electric
dams, but as they cover a huge area, they have been developed
into centres for water sports anf fishing. I stayed on a camp-site at
Le Vibal, near Salars, and had fish stewed or fried each evening,
as guests of my neighbours.

The Olt is a great fishing river. Trout abound in the clear
waters and crayfish lurk under the stones and are prodded out by
the children. The wine trade was destroyed by phylloxera and
now, apart from the tourists who come fishing, St. Geniez lives
entirely by growing strawberries. It produces enough to give a bas-
ketful away free to every passing car on the second Sunday in
June — a delightful surprise that almost makes the traffic jam
worthwhile.

North of the river, a series of minor roads lead up to the hills of Aubrac.

This, although part of the ancient Rouergue, and now the department of Aveyron and thus within our brief, is really the most southern outcrop of the Massif Central, lying between the Lot and the Truyère, the river that marks the boundary between

Bridge of 'Le Frères Pontiff, on the Olt

the Rouergue and Auvergne, and borders the Aubrac to the west. In winter the Aubrac is a snow-caked wilderness, a paradise for the cross-country ski-er and when the snow melts in the spring, the great wide pastures are a sea of flowers. I have seen the children of Aumont coming home with arms full of wild narcissi as late as June, and everywhere the hills are a riot of blue and yellow.

The Aubrac today is cattle country and in May the cows, which

The Aubrac

have spent all winter in thick-walled barns, are released to fatten themselves on the lush grass. Cattle are also still used here to pull ploughs and carts. I like the solitude of the Aubrac immensely, for while lacking the gaunt aspect of the causse, it has that vast still area of hill and sky with only the clouds moving that seems to me most restful.

Nasbinals is the centre of the Aubrac, and the site of an immense cattle market. To the southeast lies the walled town of Marvejols, which has two fine gates and two awful statues, one of the legendary Wolf of the Gévaudan, and the other of Henri IV. Marvejols was destroyed by the Catholics and rebuilt by the King's command, so the statue is supposed to be a thanks-offering. I think the King would set his own torch to the town if he saw it!

The Beast of the Gévaudan lived locally and, being an enormous wolf which enjoyed a diet of children, it soon had the district terrified. Louis XV sent his chief huntsman to chase the beast away, but it finally fell to the musket of a local hunter, after having eaten some fifty people. Perhaps wolves did survive locally into the 18th century, but given the French habit of shooting anything that moves, I rather doubt it.

142

Marvejols

The little town of Aumont-Aubrac has an excellent hotel, the *Hotel Central de la Gare*, which has every comfort and excellent food, and is not far away from such places at St. Urcize and the ski resort of Super-Blaize.

Aubrac, which gives its name to these mountains is just a little place, but it lies on the old pilgrim track and once had a garrison of soldier monks whose task was to convey the Compostella pilgrims across the Aubrac, protecting them from any wolves, human or four-footed, that might seek to prey on them. The pilgrim road here is easy to follow and clearly way-marked with the '*coquille St. Jacques*'.

From Aubrac you can follow a little road over the escarpment and down again to the Lot. The Aubrac is not a famous place, and '*Happy is the land that has no history*', but it has great beauty and if there is little to tell there is much to see.

*   *   *   *

Compostella track across the Aubrac

Where the Lot regains its name, three villages follow one another in rapid succession. They are, from the east, Espalion, Estaing and Entraygues, and they lie along the Lot within twenty-five miles of each other. If you go nowhere else in this part of France, try and visit these three place, for you won't regret it.

Espalion straddles the river and is overlooked by the picturesque ruins of the château Calmont. It has old houses by the river, is largely constructed in the dull red stone of Rodez, and has, just outside the town, the so-called *Église de Perse*. This marks the spot where St. Hilarian was martyred and is at least nine hundred years old. The tympanum is well worth inspection before you press on to Estaing.

It is best to drive through Estaing and turn to approach the town from the west, up river. That way the town, the castle and the little bridge combine into a jewel, and as I'm a great believer in first impressions, this is the best way to first see Estaing, for this first impression is breathtaking.

The river curls round the base of the town, a silver footnote to the golden walls, and the great grim castle towers over all. A walk around the town leads necessarily across a series of footbridges where the torrent of the little Cousanne rushes through the town

144

and out into the Lot. This is, or was, the seat of the ancient family of Estaing, which began in the 12th century when the founder of the house, Dieudonne, served Phillip-Augustus at the battle of Bovines, and helped to harry King John Lackland and the English out of Normandy for ever. He received Estaing as the reward for his efforts.

For the next six hundred years the family produced soldiers, sailors and churchmen in roughly even numbers. In the 16th century one, François, became Bishop of Rodez and a Saint. His feast day is still celebrated in Estaing, although, apart from his statue on the bridge, the visitor will see more frequent reminders of his unlucky descendant, Charles d'Estaing, admiral of France. The British, remembering Trafalgar and the Glorious First of June, often forget that France too has produced great seamen. Suffren and Estaing were two of them and fought and beat the British not infrequently in the Indies and Americas during the Seven Years War and the War of Independence. Estaing then left the navy and went into politics, which is never a wise move. At the Revolution, although a staunch Republican, he tried to defend Marie Antoinette and went himself to the guillotine during the Reign of Terror. "*Send my head to the English, they will be glad to see it*", was his parting shot to the judges. Castle Estaing is now a convent and the glory of the little town has quite fallen away, but you should see it all the same.

*   *   *   *

Entraygues-sur-Truyère is formidable. It lies in a deep gorge where the wide Truyère flows into the Lot, and although the Truyère is the larger stream, here it loses all identity. They have good wine in Entraygues and some strong buildings. The château stands in the middle of the town and you can walk round the walls to the point where the rivers meet and look back up their course, to the bridges. A 13th-century packhorse bridge spans the Truyère, while a series of high stepping stones gives additional passage across the Lot.

North from Entraygues lie the gorges of the Truyère, which if less famous than those of the Tarn, are no less lovely, especially where the dams have not fatally altered the nature of the country.

Below Entraygues lies another causse, the causse du Comtal, and if you cross it, heading south, you will arrive in Rodez, capital of the Rouergue.

Rodez is another red city, but in dull stone, unlike glowing Albi, or pink Toulouse. The people of Rodez, the *Ruthenois*, are

Espalion

also supposed to have red hair which, on careful inspection, I found no more prevalent there than anywhere else, and where it existed it owed as much to the bottle as to heredity.

Rodez is divided within the circling boulevards into two parts, the Cité and the Bourg. Until the Counts of Rodez died out in the 16th century, they lived in the *bourg* and contested the lordship of the town with the Bishops who occupied and fortified the Cité and cathedral. Riots and disputes between supporters of the rival powers kept the townspeople occupied when there was no other enemy to fight. When the last Count died and his lands passed to the Crown, the Bishops took the title and absorbed the *bourg*.

The cathedral, a massive building with a fine rose-window overlooking the Place d'Armes and the long Avenue Victor Hugo, was built onto the walls as part of the fortifications. The bell tower came later and was built from the revenues of his See by François d'Estaing.

Behind the cathedral, as is usually the case, lies the old quarter of the town, the usual maze of narrow streets and alleys, with

Entraygues-sur-Truyère

many medieval or Renaissance houses, and a very adequate restaurant, the *Moderne*, in Rue Abbe-Bessou. The whole town stands on a hill and so the streets are always sliding up or down, still following the course of trackways older than time. From the Square des Embergues, you can get fine views over the countryside, across the causse, and to the hills of Aubrac, before leaving for the drive across country to the Salles la Source on the road to Conques.

* * * *

Conques is a little place, barely a village. Few people have heard of it and fewer still visit it, and yet, little Conques has several claims to be ranked among one of the artistic capitals of the world, for it contains, in a setting of splendid antiquity and great natural beauty, the last remaining medieval treasure in Europe, and it is all still there because of a little girl, a thief, and a very shrewd mayor.

The little girl, Ste. Foy, was martyred for the faith, in the reign of the Diocletian and her relics were first transported to Agen, where the monks enjoyed considerable prosperity as a result.

Cathedral, Rodez

Conques

We really must look at this business of relics. It must have been a thriving business, for relics were venerated right across the spectrum of Medieval society and involved honest men and rogues, rich and poor, the devout and the excommunicated. The range of relics was almost as infinite, ranging from the Crown of Thorns, which St. Louis himself obtained from Constantinople and built a whole church, the Ste.-Chapelle in Paris to contain, to the toe-nails of the most obscure saints and martyrs. The possession of certain relics was for a church or monastery almost a guarantee of prosperity and providing the story was good enough, the provenance of the relic didn't seem to matter. The pilgrims were sure to arrive, and indeed many still do. I heard just recently, a tale of an Irish lady who went to the shrine of St. Bernadette at Lourdes where, somewhat overcome by the fatigue of the day, she lay down in one of the wheelchairs with which the town is amply provided and fell asleep. When she awoke, she was surprised to find herself among a great throng, all on their knees, praying at the shrine of Bernadette. Somewhat embarrassed she leapt up, and tried to sidle off through the crowd quietly, only to be stopped by a great outcry as everyone hailed her sudden mobility as yet

Reliquary of Ste Foy

another miracle! In the confusion she tripped over and broke an ankle, and is probably one of the few people to return from Lourdes worse than when she went there.

During the Middle Ages, it must have seemed at times that half Christendom was on the move. It must be remembered that pilgrimages were difficult to go on. Apart from the cost, the lords were reluctant to let their vassals travel away when their labour was needed on the land. Passports had to be obtained from the local Bishop, for a man without proof of his purpose could easily be arrested as a vagrant or rogue, while if he was honest, there remained the problem of robbers. All in all, it must have been the most exhausting business, but it never lacked support. Apart from the Crusaders, there were pilgrimages to Walsingham and Canterbury in England, to Rome and Assissi in Italy, to Rocamadour and Vézelay in France and to Santiago in Spain, as well as to a score of smaller places, but, at first anyway, none came to Conques.

The brethren were somewhat put out at this, for being a Clunic foundation on the Santiago road, they had to feed and house hundreds of pilgrims, but received little but thanks in return.

Then the abbot had an idea. He summoned one of the monks, Brother Aronisdus, and sent him off in secular garments to join the community of Ste. Foy at Agen. Aronisdus' orders were explicit. He was to join their community, ingratiate himself with the brethren and wait until it was his turn to guard the relics, which the monks watched closely. Then it was to be up with the relics and over the monastery wall, back to Conques as fast as his sandles would take him. Brother Aronisdus was, in modern terms, a 'sleeper'. He joined the monks at Agen and served as a brother for ten years until his turn came. His patience deserved a better cause. He grabbed the relics and fled into the night, with his brother monks and the townsfolk of Agen in hot pursuit but, so it is said, Ste. Foy herself called up a mist which concealed him from his pursuers.

Once the relics were installed at Conques they were under the protection of Cluny, who paid compensation to Agen, but kept them none the less. Pilgrims and riches descended on Conques, and over the years, a vast treasure began to fill up the Romanesque cathedral. The people of Conques themselves, each as much as he was able, gave the money for the reliquary of Ste. Foy, which is in fact hideous, and, by the early 18th century, when people ceased to go on pilgrimages, the abbey had a unique treasure, not only in sheer value, but in historical assortment. Most church treasures had, by that time, already disappeared. Rocamadour lost hers at the hands of the English in the 13th century, and when the Reformation overtook St. Thomas-à-Becket's tomb at Canterbury, it took thirty wagons to haul the gold away to King Henry's treasury. Subsequent upheavals took care of the other medieval halidoms, but safe in the hills, Conques still remained, and kept her relics.

Then came the Revolution, and word came to the village that the Committee of Public Safety from Rodez was on its way to seize the treasure. The mayor summoned the villagers and divided up the treasure among them, with instructions to hide it in the safest place they had. After the Revolution storm had passed, the items — or most of them — were recovered and can still be seen in the treasury at Conques.

It has a range of items dating from the 9th to the 16th century, often the gift of significant historical characters. It includes, apart from the gold, black-faced reliquary of Ste. Foy, an arm bone of St. George and one of the rare 'Alphabet' reliquaries of Charlemagne.

The abbey itself, which was constructed in the 11th and 12th centuries, is a vast building, with yet another of those classical tympanum over the west door. Like most tympanum, the item is a doom, or Last Judgement; Christ, as usual, sits in majesty and Ste. Foy is numbered among his attendants, while Satan welcomes the damned to his infernal kingdom.

Inside, Ste. Foy's is an interesting church. Like all pilgrim churches, the side aisles are extended into a complete ambulatory, which enabled the pilgrims to be ordered into a queue and file round the church, past the relics (and offertory box) and out again, with the minimum of fuss. The grille before the choir is unusual, for it was forged in the 12th century from the fetters of

The Street of St Jacques, Conques

prisoners released after they, or their relatives, had made an offering to Ste. Foy. The church was set on fire by the Protestants in 1561, but the heavens opened and the rain put the fires out. Perhaps Ste. Foy has influence after all, certainly over the weather. St. Swithin must be quite put out with her!

Nowadays Conques is largely deserted. There is one good hotel and two little ones, but not many people come here now and the pilgrims no longer file out of the west gate on the next stage of their march to Compostella.

* * * *

When in Aprill, the sweete showers fall
and pierce the drought of March een to the roote
... then people long to go on pilgrimage ...
and palmers long to seeke the stranger strands
of far off saynts, hallow in divers lands.

It's a strange story, the pilgrimage, and our own Chaucer for one has done very well out of it. Here we have most of the adult population of Western Europe, at some time in their lives, saving up — often for years — to travel at some risk and considerable discomfort, for months on end, from one pilgrim site to another, to a remote abbey on the sea-coast of Spain, gazing en-route at a whole series of dismembered bodies, yellow bones, or pieces of metal, wood and linen. That, plainly put, is what it all comes down to, and yet when you consider that it went on for centuries, either they were all mad or gullible, or ...

It was faith which made them do it, and in the end it is faith, and not the relic, which makes the miracle. There is little faith left today in anything, so not surprisingly there are few miracles.

* * * *

Little Conques is the last stop in our tour of the wild country beyond the Dordogne, and the road now lies north to Aurillac,

156

or, to stay as long as possible within our boundary, west across the Aubrac through Laguiole, St. Urcize and up towards St. Flour.

The Truyère, which marks the northern boundary of Rouergue is spanned at Garabit on the main north road, by a wide and beautiful bridge, which was built by Eiffel years before he put up his famous tower in Paris. Paris! Even here she has a memento. You can look back from the escarpment across the Truyère and see the lovely hills behind, but the trip is over and it is still a long way home.

Bibliography

Michelin Green Guides to:- *Auvergne, Périgord, Causses* and *Pyrénées.*
Michelin Red Guide (Current year's edition)
Guide des Logis de France (Current year's edition)
Guide de Relais-Routiers (Current year's edition)
Gods, Graves & Scholars by C.W. Ceram: Penguin
Three Rivers of France by Freda White (1954)
West of the Rhône by Freda White (1964)
The French by Sanche de Gramont: Hodder
The Dordogne by Neil Lands: Spurbooks (1975)
L'Auvergne, Debidour et Plessy (Arthaud)
Tarn-et-Garonne — Guide des Départements de France
Fastness of France by Brian Morgan
South of Toulouse by Andrew Shirley: Chatto & Windus
Topo Guide des *Sentiers de Grande Randonnée (GR65)*
    Compostella
Assemblies of Languedoc by Thomas Bisson (Princeton U.P.)
The Road to Compostella by W.F. Starkie

Index